W9-BPM-393

HOLT ASSESSMENT
Writing, Listening, and Speaking
Tests and Answer Key

Workshop Tests in Standardized Test Format
Evaluation Forms
Scales and Rubrics
Holistic Scoring Guides
6 Traits—Plus 1 Analytical Scale
Sample Papers
Portfolio Assessment

HOLT, RINEHART AND WINSTON

A Harcourt Education Company

Orlando • **Austin** • New York • San Diego • Toronto • London

STAFF CREDITS

Executive Editor:
Kristine E. Marshall

Senior Editor:
Julie Barnett Hoover

Project Editor:
Jane Kominek

Copyediting:
Michael Neibergall, *Copyediting Manager;* Kristen Azzara, Mary Malone, *Copyediting Supervisors;* Christine Altgelt, Elizabeth Dickson, Leora Harris, Anne Heausler, Kathleen Scheiner, *Senior Copyeditors;* Emily Force, Julia Thomas Hu, Nancy Shore, *Copyeditors*

Project Administration:
Marie Price, *Managing Editor;* Elizabeth LaManna, *Associate Managing Editor;* Janet Jenkins, *Senior Editorial Coordinator;* Christine Degollado, Betty Gabriel, Mark Koenig, Erik Netcher, *Editorial Coordinators*

Permissions:
Ann Farrar, *Senior Permissions Editor;* Sally Garland, Susan Lowrance, *Permissions Editors*

Design:
Betty Mintz, Richard Metzger, *Design Directors;* Chris Smith, *Senior Designer*

Production:
Beth Prevelige, *Senior Production Manager;* Carol Trammel, *Production Manager;* Belinda Barbosa Lopez, Michael Roche, *Senior Production Coordinators;* Dolores Keller, Carol Marunas, *Production Coordinators;* Myles Gorospe, *Production Assistant*

Manufacturing:
Shirley Cantrell, *Manufacturing Supervisor;* Mark McDonald, *Inventory Analyst;* Amy Borseth, *Manufacturing Coordinator*

Printed in the United States of America

ISBN 0-03-068509-5

1 2 3 4 5 6   179   06 05 04 03

Table of Contents

Table of Contents *continued*

Scales and Rubrics

for Student Edition
pp. 112–1061

An analytical scale plus
rubric for each

• Writing Workshop

• Media Workshop

• assignment in the
Speaking and
Listening Handbook

Table of Contents *continued*

Scales and Sample Papers

Portfolio Assessment

Overview of ELEMENTS OF LITERATURE Assessment Program

Two assessment booklets have been developed for ELEMENTS OF LITERATURE.

(1) Assessment of student mastery of selections and specific literary, reading, and vocabulary skills in the **Student Edition:**

  • *Holt Assessment: Literature, Reading, and Vocabulary*

(2) Assessment of student mastery of writing workshops and specific media, writing, listening, and speaking skills and assignments in the **Student Edition:**

  • *Holt Assessment: Writing, Listening, and Speaking*

Diagnostic Assessment

Holt Assessment: Literature, Reading, and Vocabulary contains two types of diagnostic tests:

• The Entry-Level Test is a diagnostic tool that helps you determine (1) how well students have mastered essential prerequisite skills needed for the year and (2) to what degree students understand the concepts that will be taught during the current year. This test uses multiple tasks to assess mastery of literary, reading, and vocabulary skills.

• The Collection Diagnostic Tests help you determine the extent of students' prior knowledge of literary, reading, and vocabulary skills taught in each collection. These tests provide vital information that will assist you in helping students master collection skills.

Holt Online Essay Scoring can be used as a diagnostic tool to evaluate students' writing proficiency:

  • For each essay, the online scoring system delivers a holistic score and analytic feedback related to five writing traits. These two scoring methods will enable you to pinpoint the strengths of your students' writing as well as skills that need improvement.

Ongoing, Informal Assessment

The **Student Edition** offers systematic opportunities for ongoing, informal assessment and immediate instructional follow-up. Students' responses to their reading; their writing, listening, and speaking projects; and their work with vocabulary skills all serve as both instructional and ongoing assessment tasks.

> **NOTE:** You may wish to address the needs of students who are reading below grade level. If so, you can administer the Diagnostic Assessment for Reading Intervention, found in the front of *Holt Reading Solutions.* This assessment is designed to identify a student's reading level and to diagnose the specific reading comprehension skills that need instructional attention.

Overview of ELEMENTS OF LITERATURE
Assessment Program *continued*

- Throughout the **Student Edition,** practice and assessment are immediate and occur at the point where skills are taught.

- In order for assessment to inform instruction on an ongoing basis, related material repeats instruction and then offers new opportunities for informal assessment.

- **Skills Reviews** at the end of each collection offer a quick evaluation of how well students have mastered the collection skills.

Progress Assessment

Students' mastery of the content of the **Student Edition** is systematically assessed in two test booklets:

- *Holt Assessment: Literature, Reading, and Vocabulary* offers a test for every selection. Multiple-choice questions focus on comprehension, the selected skills, and vocabulary development. In addition, students write answers to constructed-response prompts that test their understanding of the skills.

- *Holt Assessment: Writing, Listening, and Speaking* provides both multiple-choice questions for writing and analytical scales and rubrics for assignments in the writing and media workshops. In addition, scales and rubrics are provided for the speaking and listening skills and assignments in the Speaking and Listening Handbook in the **Student Edition**. These instruments assess proficiency in all the writing applications appropriate for each grade level.

Summative Assessment

Holt Assessment: Literature, Reading, and Vocabulary contains two types of summative tests:

- The Collection Summative Tests, which appear at the end of every collection, ask students to apply their recently acquired skills to a new literary selection. These tests contain both multiple-choice questions and constructed-response prompts.

- The End-of-Year Test helps you determine how well students have mastered the skills and concepts taught during the year. This test mirrors the Entry-Level Test and uses multiple tasks to assess mastery of literary, reading, and vocabulary skills.

Overview of ELEMENTS OF LITERATURE
Assessment Program *continued*

Holt Online Essay Scoring can be used as an end-of-year assessment tool:

- You can use *Holt Online Essay Scoring* to evaluate how well students have mastered the writing skills taught during the year. You will be able to assess student mastery using a holistic score as well as analytic feedback based on five writing traits.

Monitoring Student Progress

Both *Holt Assessment: Literature, Reading, and Vocabulary* and *Holt Assessment: Writing, Listening, and Speaking* include skills profiles that record progress toward the mastery of skills. Students and teachers can use the profiles to monitor student progress.

One-Stop Planner® CD-ROM with ExamView® Test Generator

All of the questions in this booklet are available on the *One-Stop Planner*® **CD-ROM with ExamView® Test Generator.** Use the ExamView Test Generator to customize any of the tests in this booklet and create a test unique to your classroom situation. You can then print the test or post it to the *Holt Online Assessment* area at www.myhrw.com.

Holt Online Assessment

Holt Online Assessment provides an easy way to administer tests to your students online. Students can log on to www.myhrw.com to take a test that you have created using the ExamView Test Generator, or you can assign one of the tests already available on the site: the Entry-Level, End-of-Year, and Collection Diagnostic tests from *Holt Assessment: Literature, Reading, and Vocabulary* and the Writing Workshop Tests from *Holt Assessment: Writing, Listening, and Speaking*.

About this book

This book, *Holt Assessment: Writing, Listening, and Speaking*, accompanies the ELEMENTS OF LITERATURE series and provides a variety of assessment resources. These include Writing Workshop Tests and Answer Key, Scales and Rubrics, Scales and Sample Papers, Portfolio Assessment, and a Skills Profile.

WRITING WORKSHOP TESTS AND ANSWER KEY

Every Writing Workshop in ELEMENTS OF LITERATURE has an accompanying Writing Workshop Test in a standardized test format. The test format will not only allow you to assess student performance but also will familiarize students with standardized tests and give them experience in test taking.

Each Writing Workshop Test provides a passage containing problems or errors in several or all of the following areas: content, organization, style, and conventions. Students demonstrate their understanding of the writing genre and their revising and proofreading skills by responding to multiple-choice items. Students revise elements of the genre, restructure segments of the passage, add or delete statements, refine language, and correct errors in the passage.

Answer Sheet

An Answer Sheet immediately follows the tests in this section. The Answer Sheet correspond to the answer options on a particular standardized test.

Answer Key

The Answer Key follows the Answer Sheet at the end of this section of the book. In addition to giving the correct answer, the Answer Key tells which Workshop skill is assessed by each item.

About This Book *continued*

SCALES AND RUBRICS

This section contains analytical scales and rubrics for each Writing Workshop, the Media Workshop, and each assignment in the Speaking and Listening Handbook. Both the scales and the rubrics are important teacher evaluation tools. In addition, the scales and rubrics can be used by students as learning and evaluation guides for their own work.

The **scales** include essential criteria for mastery of skills and ratings of each criterion based on a four-point scale. The **rubrics** are based on the same criteria listed in the scales. The rubrics clearly describe a student's work at each score point level for each specific criterion.

Score Point 0

On occasion, student work may be unscorable and consequently will receive a score point of zero. This may be true of writing, listening and speaking, and media assignments. The following are reasons to give a product a score of zero. The work

- is not relevant to the prompt or assignment
- is only a rewording of the prompt or assignment
- contains an insufficient amount of writing (or other mode) to determine whether it addresses the prompt or assignment
- is a copy of previously published work
- is illegible, incomprehensible, blank, or in a language other than English

About This Book *continued*

SCALES AND SAMPLE PAPERS

This section contains two different kinds of scales for assessing writing: the 6 Traits—Plus 1 Analytical Scale and Holistic Scales for fictional or autobiographical writing, responses to literature, and persuasion. Accompanying these scales are high-level, mid-level, and low-level examples of student writing. Individual evaluations, based on the analytical and holistic scales, follow each sample student paper. These scales can be used for on-demand writing or class assignments. Although this section is directed to teachers, students may also benefit from access to this section as they write and revise.

PORTFOLIO ASSESSMENT

This section begins with an essay designed to provide an introduction to portfolio work, including suggestions about how to develop and use portfolios and how to conduct conferences with students about their work.

Forms

The introductory essay is followed by a set of student forms for assessing and organizing portfolio contents and for setting goals for future work. Also included is a set of forms for communicating with parents or guardians about student work and for generally assessing students' progress.

Forms in this section can be used to record work, to establish baselines and goals, and to think critically about student work in a variety of areas. These areas include writing, listening, and speaking. The goal of these forms is to encourage students to develop criteria for assessing their own work and to identify areas for improvement. Many forms can also be used for assessment of a peer's work and for teacher evaluations.

Writing Workshop Tests and Answer Keys

for **WRITING WORKSHOP** | *page 112*

Writing Workshop: Story

DIRECTIONS Carden's teacher has asked the students to enter the short story writing contest at school. Carden has decided to write a story about someone his age.

1 **What question would be best for Carden to ask as he thinks about developing the main character?**

A Will my story contain exciting events?

B How does this character really talk?

C Will my best friend like the story?

D In the story, what sounds are heard in the house?

2 **While planning the plot of his story, Carden needs to focus MOST on—**

A the main character's parents

B dialogue he wants to include

C descriptions of all the characters

D the conflict and its resolution

This is a draft of the story Carden wrote for the contest. It contains errors in organization, development, and grammar. Use the draft to answer questions 3–10.

> As Neal put the hairpin into the fragile lock of his sister's journal, he
> (1)
> concentrated on what she had done to him. He had considered ripping
> (2)
> the lock right off the book, but he knew better. As the lock popped open,
> (3)
> undamaged, Neal congratulated himself on his perfect plan. He would
> (4)
> find some juicy secrets and pass them around school. All he could think
> (5)
> about was how his sister had borrowed his new bike and wrecked it,
>
> scratching the flawless blue paint.
>
> After he read that his sister had done a favor for him, his attitude
> (6)
> toward her changed. As he turned the pages, he found himself in a secret
> (7)
> world where he knew he didn't belong. "I shouldn't be reading this, he
> (8)
> said to himself. Along with all the other predictable secrets, he learned
> (9)
> that it was his sister, not his parents, who had taken his drawing out of the

GO ON

trash and entered it in the local contest. That's how he had won second
(10)
place and the new bike.

Just when Neal was about to close the journal, the latest entry leaped
(11)
out at him. He read, "Everything went wrong today. At Dooley's, I
(12)   (13)
dropped some really expensive nail polish I was looking at and the bottle

shattered. What a mess! I sneaked out and however believe it or not ran
(14)   (15)
Neal's bike into a tree on my way home. Somehow I have to pay for both,
(16)
but Neal loves that bike. What if it's never the same?"
(17)

Suddenly, Neal remembered why he was in her room, but it no longer
(18)
mattered.

Three days later, Neal's sister opened a letter with no return address.
(19)
She read, "I saw you break something in Dooley's last weekend. I bought a
(20)   (21)
bottle of the same polish and then left it. Here's the receipt. I am doing this
(22)   (23)
because someone once did something nice for me. A friend"
(24)

3 **Which opening sentence would MOST effectively build suspense?**

A   Neal's parents were out shopping.

B   Neal's best pal was Rusty, his Irish setter.

C   Neal sneaked into his sister's empty room.

D   The neighborhood was quiet that day.

4 **Which sentence should be moved to follow sentence 10?**

A   4

B   5

C   6

D   7

GO ON

5 In sentence 8, <u>reading this, he said</u> is best written —

A reading this" he said,

B reading this," he said

C reading this he said"

D as it is

6 In sentence 12, <u>He read, "Everything went</u> is best written—

A He read, everything went

B He read "Everything went

C He read, "everything went

D as it is

7 Which transitional word would BEST replace <u>however</u> in sentence 15 to show the order of events?

A also

B then

C first

D lately

8 Which sentence, if added after sentence 18, would make the overall message of the story clearer?

A He had learned a secret about his sister—that she was a better friend than he had realized.

B His bike was damaged, and now he would need to work to get the money to repair it.

C He would tell his sister that he knew her secret and that she did not need to worry about his bike.

D He wasn't sure he wanted to learn any more secrets about his sister, so he decided not to sneak into her room again.

9 To emphasize that the narrator knows everything about the characters, which words, if any, would be BEST added to the end of sentence 19?

A to me

B with her brother Neal

C in the privacy of her room

D No words should be added to the sentence.

10 In sentence 21, which words should replace "left it" to make the outcome of the story clear?

A used it right away

B went home

C put it back on the shelf

D didn't really want it very much

for **WRITING WORKSHOP** | page 222 | **TEST**

Writing Workshop: Problem-Solution Essay

DIRECTIONS Lucinda's class has been asked to write an essay describing a problem and offering a solution. Lucinda wants to get her essay published in the school newspaper.

1 **Which question would BEST help Lucinda choose a topic?**

  A What examples do I want to include in my essay?

  B Where can I find background information about my topic?

  C What problem would I like to do something about?

  D Who do I know that has a serious problem?

2 **When deciding on her audience, Lucinda MOST needs to consider—**

  A visitors from other schools who might pick up the school newspaper

  B people who can help with the solution to the problem

  C adults who graduated from her school twenty or more years ago

  D people who already agree with her opinion about the problem

Here is a draft of Lucinda's essay. It contains errors in development, organization, and grammar. Use the draft to answer questions 3–10.

> Over the summer, I visited my cousin in another state. When she asked
> (1)   (2)
> me if I wanted to see her yearbook, I said, "Sure!" She promptly popped
>   (3)
> a tape into the VCR, and I watched a yearbook full of color, action, inter-
>
> views, and music. Our school should produce a video yearbook instead of
>   (4)
> a print yearbook.
>
>   Video does a completer job of portraying people and events than still
>   (5)
> photography. My cousin's yearbook captured the band playing the school
>   (6)
> fight song. No print yearbook can do that. Video also allows viewers to see
>   (7)   (8)
> a bigger picture of an event. Suppose the basketball team gets carried
>   (9)
> away. A video yearbook can capture the sound of the buzzer, the roar of
>   (10)
> the crowd, and the happy celebrating of the team. Print yearbooks just
>   (11)
> cannot compete with moving pictures and sound to capture excitement
>
> and emotion.

GO ON ▶

Video yearbooks also cost less than print yearbooks. The cost of printing (12) (13) continues to rise, but the cost of technology is decreasing. Overtown (14) Middle School's video yearbook cost twenty dollars. Students and parents (15) both like to save money.

Producing a video yearbook also teaches students how to put their best (16) foot forward with technology. Students learn how to film, edit, and use (17) graphics to make an effective video. Mike Gieger, president of Gieger (18) Enterprises, says, "Multimedia presentations are becoming more important in business all the time. My employees need to know how to use this tech- (19) nology." Producing a video yearbook would give students an opportunity (20) to learn these multimedia skills.

A print yearbook may soon be as outdated as a typewriter. After all, it is (21) (22) hard to compete against a popular video yearbook.

3 To grab the reader's attention, which sentence would BEST replace sentence 1?

A   My cousin had a surprise for me.

B   My cousin had something to share with me.

C   Over the summer, I got a good idea from my cousin.

D   My cousin couldn't wait to show me her newest treasure.

4 Which sentence should be added following sentence 3 to state the problem clearly?

A   Technology can make a yearbook more exciting.

B   I was impressed with the quality of my cousin's yearbook.

C   Students can learn something from helping to produce a video yearbook.

D   Our school's print yearbooks are dull and expensive.

GO ON

5 **What is the BEST way to revise sentence 5?**

A   Video does a more complete job of portraying people and events than still photography does.

B   Video does a completer job of portraying people and events.

C   Video is completer at portraying people and events than still photography does.

D   Video does a job of portraying people and events than still photography.

6 **Which sentence would BEST follow sentence 13?**

A   Many books cost more than videotapes.

B   Most of us don't have a lot of money to waste.

C   Our yearbook with fifty-six pages cost twenty-eight dollars.

D   Would you rather have an exciting video or a boring book?

7 **Which of the following represents the best revision of sentence 16?**

A   Producing a video yearbook also teaches students how to sink or swim with technology.

B   Producing a video yearbook also teaches students how to climb the ladder of success with technology.

C   Producing a video yearbook also teaches students how to communicate effectively with technology.

D   Producing a video yearbook also teaches students how to come through with flying colors with technology.

8 **Which sentence should be added following sentence 20?**

A   Employers expect their employees to have skills in using technology.

B   Most important, gaining these skills will prepare students for future jobs.

C   Also, the video yearbook will be cheaper, and more students can buy it.

D   If we take good care of it, the video might even last longer than a book.

9 **Which sentence, if added before sentence 21, would BEST address possible objections?**

A   Video yearbooks are more modern than print yearbooks, so most people soon will prefer the videos.

B   It is true that a video yearbook is not practical if you want to look at it outdoors.

C   People may miss turning the pages of print yearbooks, but video yearbooks bring sound and movement to school history.

D   Videos are so popular that video yearbooks will probably replace print yearbooks.

10 **What is the BEST sentence to add to the end of the essay as a call to action?**

A   Let's write a plan for a video yearbook and make next year's yearbook the most exciting ever.

B   I want to hear from anyone who might be willing to help.

C   Even if you don't want to work on the yearbook, you might have some good ideas.

D   Next year's yearbook can be the best our school has ever had if we change from print to video.

Writing Workshop: Personal Narrative

DIRECTIONS Jamal's teacher has asked his students to write a narrative about an experience they have had. Jamal wants to write about an experience from which he learned something.

1 **Which question will BEST help Jamal choose a subject for his narrative?**

A   Where did the experience occur?

B   Were family members involved in the experience?

C   Do I remember the experience clearly?

D   How will I organize my personal narrative?

2 **After choosing a subject, Jamal should first write—**

A   the descriptive details he will use

B   a statement of why the experience is important

C   an outline of events

D   dialogue that he will use to reveal character

Here is Jamal's draft. The draft contains errors in development, organization, and grammar. Use the draft to answer questions 3–10.

Never Too Old

Until last month, when I witnessed something at a gym that made me
(1)
see my grandmother in a completely different light, I thought only of the

attention she always gives me, the special presents she chooses for me, and

her great cooking. Over the years, I had heard hints about Grandma's other
(2)
activities. However, I was so busy thinking about what Grandma was
(3)
doing for me or giving me that I hadn't thought about what else she might

like to do.

Last month, Mom and Dad told me that we had a special event to go to
(4)
on a Saturday. Mom and Dad wouldn't tell me what we were going to do,
(5)
just that it would be at a gym.

That Saturday, we left the house with an ice chest full of sandwiches and
(6)
bottled water. We pulled into the parking lot of a high school gym. While
(7)   (8)
Mom drove, I took a nap, not really caring where we were going. When I
(9)

GO ON ➡

woke up, I realized that we were in the town where Grandma lives. I still
(10)

didn't have a clue. I noticed that lots of people were wearing white pants.
(11)

As they walked into the gym, Jamal saw children, teenagers, and adults
(12)

putting on white jackets and colored belts.

What are we doing here? I asked. Mom just smiled.
(13)   (14)

Mom, Dad, and I sat down on the bleachers. I saw Mom and Dad
(15)   (16)

exchange a look. I was just bored. I looked at the gym floor, which was
(17)   (18)

divided into squares. In the square nearest us, several women were lined
(19)

up. They were wearing protective equipment. One of the women had the
(20)   (21)

name "Chapman" embroidered on the back of her jacket. That's my last
(22)

name, but it isn't an unusual name.

That woman and another woman walked to the center of their square,
(23)

were stepping behind taped lines on the floor, and bowed to the referee

and then to each other. After reminding the women to make just light con-
(24)

tact, the referee told them to begin. They began kicking and jabbing at each
(25)

other. Ms. Chapman landed a kick on her opponent's side. Now I wasn't
(26)   (27)

bored. Ms. Chapman sidestepped a kick and landed a punch on the side
(28)

of her opponent's headgear. Next, the other woman landed a kick. Still,
(29)   (30)

Ms. Chapman ended up winning the bout.

Imagine my surprise when the women took off their headgear and I
(31)

recognized Grandma! I knew that she had been taking some kind of fitness
(32)

classes, but I hadn't paid much attention. Watching Grandma spar has not
(33)

only given me a different view of her and caused me to pay more attention

to what interests her, but it has changed my view of adults.

GO ON

3 Which sentence should be added to the beginning of the narrative?

A   My personal narrative will be about my grandmother.

B   I had a hard time thinking of a subject, but I finally decided on one.

C   My grandmother has always been very good to me.

D   What picture comes to your mind when you hear the word *grandma*?

4 Sentence 7 should be moved to follow sentence—

A   5

B   8

C   9

D   11

5 In sentence 12, how should
As they walked into the gym, Jamal saw be written?

A   As they walked into the gym, he saw

B   As Jamal walked into the gym, they saw

C   As we walked into the gym, I saw

D   As I walked into the gym, they saw

6 How should sentence 13 be written?

A   "What are we doing here? I asked."

B   "What are we doing here?" I asked.

C   "What are we doing here"? I asked.

D   'What are we doing here? I asked.'

7 In sentence 20, what is the BEST way to write protective equipment?

A   equipment that would protect them

B   padded protective gear

C   sparring equipment to protect the head from hits or kicks

D   bright red and gold protective headgear and padded gloves and boots

8 What is the BEST way to change sentence 23?

A   Change **walked** to **were walking**

B   Change **were stepping** to **stepped**

C   Change **bowed** to **were bowing**

D   Change **walked** to **had walked**

9 Which sentence should replace sentence 27 to make Jamal's feelings clearer?

A   Now, I was interested in what was happening in the gym.

B   My parents knew what they were doing that day.

C   Suddenly, I was excitedly cheering Ms. Chapman.

D   I wasn't bored anymore, as I had been when we entered the gym.

10 Which sentence should be added to the end of the essay?

A   Other students may have missed some interesting events.

B   Grandma is very important to me, and I will always appreciate her.

C   We should all try to keep physically fit, no matter how old we are.

D   Now I plan to make an extra effort to learn from their experiences.

for **WRITING WORKSHOP** | page 462 | **TEST**

Writing Workshop: Descriptive Essay

DIRECTIONS Gabriella's teacher has asked the students to write a descriptive essay about something they have observed.

1 **Which question will BEST help Gabriella identify a good subject for her descriptive essay?**

A Where can I publish an essay on this subject?

B Will my friends enjoy reading about my subject?

C Does the subject involve enough sensory details for a good description?

D Do I know other people who can provide information about the subject?

2 **Which question will BEST help Gabriella determine the main idea of her essay?**

A How can I research this subject?

B What is my overall impression of my subject?

C What is the best way to organize my sensory details?

D What figurative language should I include in my essay?

Here is a draft of Gabriella's essay. It contains errors in development, organization, and grammar. Use the draft to answer questions 3–10.

Ice Day

Though some people get to see ice and snow all winter, we hardly ever
(1)
get to see them where I live. When grass; twigs; bushes, and ordinary
(2)
objects are covered in ice, you can see these things in a different way.

How often have you noticed the veins in a leaf? Ice can show details of
(3)   (4)
things. I had not paid much attention to these details until we had our first
(5)
ice storm in several years. From the living-room window, I could see a
(6)
white wonderland. At the same time, I smelled the bread that my father
(7)
was baking. Ice pellets, sleet, and even some snowflakes covered every-
(8)
thing. No footprint messed up the glistening surface. It was as though
(9)   (10)
someone had iced the yard, the sidewalks, and the parking lot with

cake frosting.

GO ON ➡

Ice had even blown around the door to my family's apartment on the
(11)
third floor. Icicles hung from the handrail, and ice covered the stairs. A
(12)   (13)
sheet of ice stretched from the foot of the stairs all the way to the sidewalk

and yard and into the parking lot. The cars had sheets of ice over their
(14)
windshields and heaps of ice pellets on their hoods. Sheets of ice also cov-
(15)
ered the side windows. Icicles hung from the branches of the trees, each
(16)
icicle ending in a small bulb. Before, I had not noticed the structure of the
(17)
trees. I noticed that they looked like charcoal sketches. Ice frosted the roof,
(18)   (19)
drifting like sand.

My four-year-old sister had never seen an icy scene before. She said,
(20)   (21)
"See, ice cream leaf, ice stick." She was so excited that I had to stop her
(22)
before she ran outside without her coat, hat, and gloves. After she was
(23)
warmly bundled up, I took her outside. She kept picking up ice-covered
(24)
leaves and twigs and bringing them to me. Our cat, Sylvester, wasn't so
(25)
pleased. He hissed when his paws first touched the ice. Then, when his
(26)   (27)
nose touched the ice, he sniffed the grass and jumped back. Some small ice
(28)
pellets were still falling as we stood outside. With his hair fluffed out,
(29)
Sylvester looked like a glass ornament as tiny ice pellets stuck to the ends

of his hair. When we all went back inside, <u>the lights make</u> the ice pellets
(30)
on Sylvester's hair shine and change colors. Who would have thought my
(31)
cat could look like a modern sculpture?

The ice helped me notice things I had never paid attention to before. It
(32)   (33)
helped me understand how photographers think of using ordinary objects

for artistic photos. It may be several more years before we see another icy
(34)
wonderland in South Texas.

GO ON

3 **Which sentence should be added after sentence 1 to identify the subject clearly?**

A　Up North, people get to see ice and snow many times every winter.

B　Last week we had a rare chance to see an icy landscape in South Texas.

C　Many of us are happy when we finally get to see ice and snow.

D　Some of us are lucky to see snow once every seven or eight years.

4 **What is the BEST way to write grass; twigs; bushes, and ordinary objects in sentence 2?**

A　grass, twigs, bushes, and ordinary objects

B　grass, twigs, bushes; and ordinary objects

C　grass and twigs and bushes and ordinary objects

D　grass; twigs; bushes; and ordinary objects

5 **What is the BEST way to write sentence 4 to add sensory details?**

A　The veins are harder to see during spring, when everything is green.

B　Most us do not look closely at leaves unless something unusual happens.

C　Ice can make details clearer and more noticeable.

D　A light etching of ice can highlight the faint lines in a leaf.

6 **Which sentence should be deleted from the second paragraph?**

A　7

B　8

C　9

D　10

7 **Which transitional word should be added to sentence 18 to make the chronological order clearer?**

A　Also

B　Mainly

C　Now

D　Below

8 **To make the order of the essay clearer, sentence 21 should be moved to follow sentence—**

A　22

B　23

C　24

D　25

9 **What is the BEST way to write the lights make in sentence 30?**

A　the lights were making

B　the lights made

C　the lights has made

D　the lights is making

10 **Which clause, if added to the end of sentence 34, would BEST explain why the experience is important?**

A　and we will be happy when that happens again

B　but I will not forget how cold the weather was and how I longed for summer to arrive

C　and I am sure that Sylvester hopes he never again has to go outside when it's icy

D　but I will always remember how the ice helped me to see my surroundings better

Writing Workshop: Supporting an Interpretation

DIRECTIONS Robert's teacher has asked the class to write an essay supporting an interpretation of a literary work. Robert wants to write about a poem by Paula Gunn Allen.

1 To help him sort out his thoughts and reach conclusions about his topic, Robert can BEST jot down his thoughts in—

A   an essay framework

B   an outline

C   chronological order

D   a cluster diagram

2 Before writing his essay, Robert needs to make sure that he has evidence—

A   that will fill two or three pages

B   of several different kinds

C   to support his thesis

D   that will leave readers with something to consider

Here is Robert's draft. It contains errors in development, organization, and grammar. Use the draft to answer questions 3–10.

Poetic Surprise

Sometimes, a poem can surprise you. What picture comes to your mind
(1)   (2)
when you hear the words "Indian ruins"? The reader of one of Paula Gunn
                                        (3)
Allen's poems is surprised several times. These surprises make the reader
                                        (4)
think about things differently.

Even though the title of the poem doesn't obviously refer to American
(5)
Indians, the dedication "for Joe Bruchac" leads the reader to believe that

the ruins referred to in the title are American Indian ruins. The narrator
                                        (6)
knows that the visitor wants to see the usual tourist sites of New Mexico,

so the reader isnt surprised when the narrator asks the visitor whether he

wants to see some ruins.

The narrator acknowledges that the visitor probably thinks he's going to
(7)
see sacred caves, abandoned ruins, and empty pueblos. The reader will
                                        (8)
suspect something, because the narrator drives only a few blocks and

stops at a high-security apartment building. After the narrator and the
                                        (9)

visitor enter the building, the descriptions of its interior hint at a connection to "ruins" that tourists visit.

Finally, they enter "the chic apartment." The reader and the visitor,
(10)   (11)
"Joe," are surprised when the narrator says, "I'd like you to meet the old Indian ruins / I promised. / My mother, Mrs. Francis, and my grandmother, Mrs. Gottlieb." The reader is just as surprised as the visitor. Even
(12)   (13)
though Joe is probably Joe Bruchac, an American Indian himself, he has had the same ideas that other tourists have about Indian ruins in the West. Bruchac's family is from the Abenaki people of New York, so in many
(14)
ways he's like any other tourist when he visits New Mexico.

For the reader who makes the connection between the Joe in the poem
(15)
and Joe Bruchac for whom the poem is written, the last sentence is a sly comment on Bruchac's writing. The narrator says that Joe is "still telling
(16)
the tale of the old / Indian ruins he visited in New Mexico." This implies
(17)
that Bruchac is using this story in his own writing. The narrator's final
(18)
simile compares the lifestyle of her mother and grandmother to that of ancient pueblo Indians. Two modern American Indian writers, Joe Bruchac
(19)
and the poet, are writing about two American Indian women, who, even though they live in a high-rise apartment building, live very much as their ancestors did.

Paula Gunn Allen uses sly humor to lead readers to reflect on their
(20)
views about the lives of American Indians, past and present.

GO ON ▶

WRITING WORKSHOP TESTS

3 **What is the BEST way to write sentence 3?**

A One of Paula Gunn Allen's poems surprises the reader several times.

B Among poems that surprise the reader is one by Paula Gunn Allen.

C I'm going to write about a surprising poem by Paula Gunn Allen.

D Paula Gunn Allen's poem "Taking a Visitor to See the Ruins" surprises the reader several times.

4 **What is the BEST way to write sentence 4 to make the thesis statement clear?**

A These surprises make the reader want to read more poems by this poet.

B The surprises make the reader think differently about stereotypes.

C These surprises help readers understand American Indian culture.

D A reader from New Mexico probably wouldn't be surprised by the poem.

5 **Which supporting evidence would BEST follow sentence 5?**

A Bruchac has received many awards for his writing.

B I have read several other books by Bruchac.

C Bruchac is a well-known American Indian writer.

D Bruchac has written many books for children and young people.

6 **How should isnt in sentence 6 be written?**

A isnt'

B isn't

C is'nt

D *As it is.*

7 **In sentence 6, what is the BEST way to write asks the visitor whether he wants to see some ruins. ?**

A asks, "Would you like to go see some old Indian ruins?"

B asks him whether or not he would like to visit some Indian ruins.

C says she asked the visitor if he wants to visit some ruins.

D suggests that they visit some old Indian ruins.

8 **In sentence 8, how should will suspect be written?**

A is suspecting

B will have suspected

C suspected

D suspects

9 **Which sentence would BEST follow sentence 17?**

A Bruchac has written many stories about the lives of American Indians.

B Bruchac has worked as a teacher as well as a writer.

C Of course, the poet herself is using the same story in her poem.

D Allen herself was born in New Mexico.

10 **Which sentence would BEST be added to the conclusion?**

A She undermines stereotypes and links ancient and modern lives.

B This poem made me laugh, so I'm going to read more of Allen's poems.

C Many books about American Indians have been published.

D Maybe Allen will write another poem about a visit by Bruchac.

for **WRITING WORKSHOP** | *page 772* | **TEST**

Writing Workshop: Comparison-Contrast Essay

DIRECTIONS Elizabeth's teacher has asked the students to write an essay comparing and contrasting two literary elements, subjects, or works. Elizabeth has decided to compare the novel *Holes* to an African folk tale.

1 Elizabeth can collect ideas about how the two works are alike and different by using—

    A   an outline

    B   a framework for her essay

    C   reviews of the novel

    D   a Venn diagram

2 Before beginning to write her essay, Elizabeth needs to decide whether to organize it by—

    A   chronological or reverse chronological order

    B   increasing or decreasing order of importance

    C   the block method or the point-by-point method

    D   random order or date of publication

Here is Elizabeth's draft. It contains errors in development, organization, and grammar. Use the draft to answer questions 3–10.

Hidden Treasure

Things are not always as they seem, and treasure can be found in
(1)
unlikely places. Sometimes, you may not realize what the real treasure is.
(2)
Both Louis Sacher's novel *Holes* and an African folk tale retold by Kathleen
(3)
Arnott look at this idea. Both works share themes but handle them in dif-
(4)
ferent ways.

    Both works include a main character who doesn't exactly fit in. In *Holes*,
(5)   (6)
Stanley Yelnats IV, who is a middle school student, is overweight. The
                                                  (7)
other students tease him, and he has no friends. The main character of <u>The</u>
                                                  (8)
<u>Snake King</u> is Temba, a tree cutter. He works faster than the other tree cut-
                                             (9)
ters, and he teases the others because they are slow. They envy him.
                                             (10)
Stanley believes that a curse has been put on his family because his great-
(11)
grandfather did not keep a promise to Madame Zeroni, an Egyptian

---

fortuneteller. Bad luck has followed the Yelnats family ever since then.
(12)
Temba's own behavior partly causes his bad luck. The way Temba acts
(13) **(14)**
increases the other tree cutters' envy and causes them to mistreat him.

When Stanley is sent to a juvenile detention camp, he is forced to dig
(15)
holes in an old lake bed. He figures out that the warden of the camp is
(16)
using the boys at the camp to help her find a treasure. Eventually, Stanley
(17)
finds a suitcase that belonged to his great-grandfather. In contrast, Temba
(18)
accidently finds an underground pit in which honey is stored. He shares
(19)
this treasure with the other tree cutters, and they sell the honey. When the
(20)
honey is gone, though, the other tree cutters leave Temba in the pit.

Temba finds a way to escape the pit by watching a scorpion. The Snake
(21) **(22)**
King befriends Temba and has his soldiers show Temba the way home.

Stanley's experience is somewhat different. He and his friend Zero are left
(23) **(24)**
in a hole that contains a nest of poisonous lizards. However, the lizards do
(25)
not attack him or Zero. Finally, the boys are rescued.
(26)
Though Stanley doesn't know it at the time, the curse on his family is
(27)
lifted when he carries Zero up a mountain. By helping Zero, Stanley has
(28)
fulfilled the promise his great-grandfather made to Madam Zeroni.

Temba's story doesn't have such a clear happy ending. After Temba returns
(29) **(30)**
home, the wise men torture him until he leads them to the palace of the

Snake King, where they kill the Snake King. Following the instructions the
(31)
Snake King gave him, Temba carries the body of the Snake King to a partic-

ular stream and throws the body into it. This revives the Snake King, but
(32)
the villagers will always be a threat to him if they learn that he is alive.

In both stories, an act of kindness and the fulfillment of a promise help
(33)
to lift a curse or make up for the bad deeds of others.

GO ON

3 What information should be added to sentence 3?

   A   the names of the main characters

   B   the title of the folk tale

   C   the publishers of both books

   D   the title of the book of folk tales

4 What is the BEST way to write sentence 4 to make the main idea clear?

   A   Both works share the themes of friendship and hidden treasure, but they handle them differently.

   B   Both works share certain elements but handle the themes differently.

   C   Both works are about the idea of treasure and what it means.

   D   Both works develop similar themes, but one is a novel and the other is a folk tale.

5 In sentence 8, how should The Snake King be written?

   A   *The Snake King*

   B   'The Snake King'

   C   "The Snake King"

   D   *As it is.*

6 Which transitional word or phrase should be added to sentence 13?

   A   In addition

   B   Then

   C   Similarly

   D   In contrast

7 In sentence 18, how should accidently be written?

   A   acidently

   B   accidentally

   C   acidentally

   D   *As it is.*

8 Which sentence should be added after sentence 21 to provide specific details?

   A   For a while, Temba thinks the other tree cutters are playing a joke.

   B   Temba calls for help, but no one is looking for him.

   C   He finds a tunnel that leads him to the Snake King's palace.

   D   Temba tries to get out of the pit the way he got in, but he has no rope.

9 Which detail would BEST be added after sentence 27?

   A   Carrying Zero up the mountain was a superhuman feat.

   B   Zero is the great-great-grandson of Madam Zeroni.

   C   Stanley didn't want to leave his friend behind.

   D   Zero is the first friend Stanley has ever had.

10 Which sentence should BEST be added to the conclusion?

   A   Stanley and Temba learn that friendship is worth more than gold.

   B   One story is a novel and one a folk tale, but they are similar.

   C   Temba is still an outsider at the end of the folk tale.

   D   Some people use their power to take advantage of others.

for **WRITING WORKSHOP**   *page 864*   **TEST**

Writing Workshop: Informative Report

DIRECTIONS Kanetra's teacher has asked the students in her technology class to write an informative report. Kanetra has decided to write about virtual reality.

1 **Which question will BEST help Kanetra choose sources for her report?**

A   Is the information in the source presented in an eye-catching way?

B   Can other students in my class find the same information?

C   Does the source include graphs and photographs?

D   Is the information in the source trustworthy?

2 **Before preparing an outline, Kanetra needs to decide—**

A   how she will capture her readers' attention

B   how she will organize the information in her report

C   which sources she will include in the Works Cited list

D   which media she will use in an oral presentation of her information

Here is a draft of Kanetra's informative report. It contains errors in development, organization, and grammar. Use the draft to answer questions 3–10.

Virtual Reality

Imagine taking a field trip to Mars or going inside the human heart.
(1)
Does this sound impossible? With virtual reality, you may soon be taking
(2)   (3)
these kinds of field trips. In fact, researchers are discovering new ways to
(4)
use virtual reality in medicine.

According to one definition, virtual reality is "a computer-created envi-
(5)
ronment that simulates real-life situations." In other words, a computer
(6)
allows a viewer to see, hear, feeling, and moving around in a world that

seems very real. To experience virtual reality, people must wear special
(7)
helmets, gloves, or glasses.

Virtual reality already helps many people do their jobs better. Virtual
(8)   (9)
reality helps doctors practice surgery and other risky procedures without

jeopardizing real patients. Some experts predict that medical students will
(10)

GO ON

one day study anatomy by dissecting virtual bodies instead of cadavers.

    Police in England are experimenting with a virtual reality system that
(11)
helps them look at crime scenes in a new way. Police asked researchers to
(12)
re-create a garage where a murder took place. By using special 3-D glasses,
(13)
the detectives were able to "fly" around the garage. They could look at the
(14)
scene from different angles and see what different witnesses could actually

see while the crime is being committed.

    Virtual reality is taking instant replay one step further. A viewer can use
(15)   (16)
a new program called Virtual Replay to fabricate the field and calculate the

whereabouts of the players. A viewer can enter the scene, which is three
(17)
dimensional, and look at the play from any angle or camera point. A
(18)
referee who used instant replay was limited to just a couple of camera

angles.

    Virtual reality was once used only for entertainment.
(19)

Works Cited

Grumet, Tobey. "TV Sports: The Next Dimension." Popular Mechanics

    1 Mar. 1998, p. 69.

Briggs, John. "The Promise of Virtual Reality." The Futurist 1 Sept. 1996.

Hargrave, Sean. "Fighting Crime in 3-D Mode." The Toronto Star

    28 Feb. 1999.

GO ON

3 **What is the BEST way to rewrite the thesis statement in sentence 4?**

A   In fact, researchers think this exciting new technology can change education.

B   Virtual reality is changing the ways researchers look at how police do their jobs.

C   In fact, researchers are discovering many practical uses for this exciting technology.

D   Medicine is using research in the field of virtual reality to train doctors and students.

4 **How should to see, hear, feeling, and moving in sentence 6 be written?**

A   to see, to hear, will feel, and will move

B   sees, hears, feeling, and moving

C   to see, hear, feel, and move

D   seeing, hearing, feeling, and moving

5 **What is the BEST change, if any, to make to improve the organization of paragraph 4 (sentences 11 –14)?**

A   Add a main idea statement.

B   Delete the first sentence.

C   Delete the last sentence.

D   Make no change.

6 **How should is being committed in sentence 14 be written?**

A   will be committed

B   was being committed

C   is committed

D   will have been committed

7 **Which sentence should be added to the beginning of paragraph 5?**

A   Virtual reality will make hobbies and sports even more popular.

B   Virtual reality provides viewers a new level of watching sports.

C   Computer programs simulate action, but people prefer seeing live action.

D   Soon activities may be viewed only on computer screens.

8 **What is the BEST change, if any, to make to sentence 18?**

A   A referee, who used instant replay, could decide whether or not a call was correct.

B   A referee who uses Virtual Replay would not be limited to just a couple of camera angles but could see the play from many directions.

C   A referee, who called plays with instant replay could get the same results with Virtual Replay.

D   Make no change.

9 **What is the BEST way for Kanetra to improve the conclusion of her report?**

A   Add a sentence that captures the reader's attention.

B   Include more facts and statistics.

C   Sum up her overall findings.

D   Refer to all of her sources.

10 **What is the BEST format change, if any, to make to the Works Cited list?**

A   Remove the underlines.

B   Delete the periods after the names.

C   Put the entries in alphabetical order.

D   Make no change.

Answer Sheet

Collection _____

Writing Workshop

1 Ⓐ Ⓑ Ⓒ Ⓓ 5 Ⓐ Ⓑ Ⓒ Ⓓ 9 Ⓐ Ⓑ Ⓒ Ⓓ
2 Ⓐ Ⓑ Ⓒ Ⓓ 6 Ⓐ Ⓑ Ⓒ Ⓓ 10 Ⓐ Ⓑ Ⓒ Ⓓ
3 Ⓐ Ⓑ Ⓒ Ⓓ 7 Ⓐ Ⓑ Ⓒ Ⓓ
4 Ⓐ Ⓑ Ⓒ Ⓓ 8 Ⓐ Ⓑ Ⓒ Ⓓ

Answer Key

Collection 1 Writing Workshop

p. 3 | Story

1. B (prewriting, developing main character)
2. D (prewriting, plot elements, conflict and resolution)
3. C (suspense)
4. C (building suspense)
5. B (punctuating dialogue)
6. D (punctuating and capitalizing dialogue)
7. B (transitional words to show order)
8. A (overall message of story)
9. C (point of view)
10. C (resolution)

Collection 2 Writing Workshop

p. 6 | Problem-Solution Essay

1. C (prewriting, choosing a topic)
2. B (prewriting, targeting an audience)
3. D (grabbing the reader's attention)
4. D (stating the problem)
5. A (using comparatives)
6. C (using details to describe the problem)
7. C (avoiding clichés)
8. A (elaborating on the solution)
9. C (addressing objections)
10. A (call to action)

Collection 3 Writing Workshop

p. 9 | Personal Narrative

1. C (prewriting, choosing a subject)
2. B (prewriting, statement about importance of experience)
3. D (grabbing the reader's attention)
4. C (clear order of events)
5. C (consistent point of view)
6. B (punctuating dialogue)
7. D (descriptive details)
8. B (consistent verb tenses)
9. C (writer's feelings)
10. D (conclusion, why experience is important)

Collection 4 Writing Workshop

p. 12 | Descriptive Essay

1. C (prewriting, choosing a subject)
2. B (prewriting, focusing on main idea)
3. B (introduction, identifying subject)
4. A (commas in series)
5. D (sensory details)
6. A (editing, deleting irrelevant details)
7. C (transitional words to show chronological order)
8. C (organization, clear order)
9. B (consistent verb tenses)
10. D (conclusion, importance of subject)

Answer Key *continued*

Collection 5 Writing Workshop

p. 15 | Supporting an Interpretation

1. D (prewriting, using a cluster diagram to sort ideas)
2. C (prewriting, developing a thesis)
3. D (introduction, including title of literary work)
4. B (thesis statement)
5. C (supporting evidence)
6. B (apostrophes)
7. A (using quotations from the work as evidence)
8. D (consistent verb tenses)
9. C (elaborating with commentary on quotations)
10. A (conclusion, applying thesis to a broader experience)

Collection 6 Writing Workshop

p. 18 | Comparison-Contrast Essay

1. D (prewriting, using a Venn diagram to collect ideas)
2. C (prewriting, organization)
3. B (introduction, including title of literary works)
4. A (main idea)
5. C (punctuating titles)
6. D (transitional words or phrases to show differences)
7. B (spelling)
8. C (specific details from literary works)
9. B (specific details from literary works)
10. A (conclusion, expanding on main idea)

Collection 7 Writing Workshop

p. 21 | Informative Report

1. D (prewriting, evaluating sources)
2. B (prewriting, outlining)
3. C (thesis statement)
4. C (consistent verb tenses)
5. D (organization)
6. B (consistent verb tenses)
7. B (developing subtopics in separate paragraphs)
8. B (supporting evidence)
9. C (conclusion, summing up overall findings)
10. C (formatting Works Cited list)

Scales and Rubrics

Writing: Story

Use the chart below (and the rubric on page 29) to evaluate a short story. Circle the numbers that best indicate how well the criteria are met. With eight criteria, the lowest possible score is 0, the highest 32.

4 = Clearly meets this criterion

3 = Makes a serious effort to meet this criterion and is fairly successful

2 = Makes some effort to meet this criterion but with little success

1 = Does not achieve this criterion

0 = Unscorable

CRITERIA FOR EVALUATION	RATING
Genre, Organization, and Focus	
Story has an interesting plot with an effective beginning.	4 3 2 1 0
Point of view is consistent throughout story.	4 3 2 1 0
Characters are complex and realistic.	4 3 2 1 0
Story has a definite setting.	4 3 2 1 0
Story is well organized and coherent.	4 3 2 1 0
Transitional words and phrases show the order of events.	4 3 2 1 0
Writing Conventions	
Standard English spelling, punctuation, capitalization, and manuscript form are used appropriately for this grade level.	4 3 2 1 0
Standard English grammar and sentence structure are used appropriately for this grade level.	4 3 2 1 0
Total Points:	

Writing: Story

CRITERIA FOR EVALUATION	SCORE POINT 4	SCORE POINT 3	SCORE POINT 2	SCORE POINT 1
Genre, Organization, and Focus				
Story has an interesting plot with an effective beginning.	Story has an interesting plot with an effective beginning, a conflict, complications, a suspenseful climax, and a clear resolution.	Story has a plot that includes all elements, including a somewhat appealing beginning, but some elements need more development.	Story includes most plot elements, but some elements are not clear.	Beginning does not relate to rest of story, suspense is ruined, and/or major plot elements are missing.
Point of view is consistent throughout story.	Point of view (first or third person) is clear and consistent throughout the story.	Point of view (first or third person) is consistent in most sections of story.	Point of view (first or third person) shifts periodically in story.	Point of view is inconsistent and confusing.
Characters are complex and realistic.	Characters seem to come alive and are complex and realistic.	Characters seem real; there are few instances where more detail, description, or dialogue is needed.	Characters seem real occasionally.	Characters are undeveloped, with little detail, description, or dialogue.
Story has a definite setting.	Story has a definite setting established with descriptive details.	Story has a setting that is reasonably clear.	Story has a setting that is only mentioned.	Story does not include a setting.
Story is well organized and coherent.	All events in story are well organized and coherent.	Most events in story are in order and understandable.	Some events that are out of order make it difficult for readers to understand story.	Events are in random order.
Transitional words and phrases show the order of events.	Well-chosen transitional words and phrases show the order of events throughout the story.	Transitional words and phrases usually show the order of events, leaving few gaps for the reader to fill.	Transitional words and phrases only occasionally show the order of events; some are used inappropriately.	Missing transitional words and phrases make it hard for the reader to follow the story.

CRITERIA FOR EVALUATION	SCORE POINT 4	SCORE POINT 3	SCORE POINT 2	SCORE POINT 1
Writing Conventions				
Standard English spelling, punctuation, capitalization, and manuscript form are used appropriately for this grade level.	Standard English spelling, punctuation, capitalization, and manuscript form are used appropriately for this grade level throughout the story.	Standard English spelling, punctuation, capitalization, and manuscript form are used appropriately for this grade level, with few problems.	Inconsistent use of standard English spelling, punctuation, capitalization, and manuscript form disrupts readers' comprehension.	Minimal use of standard English spelling, punctuation, capitalization, and manuscript form confuses readers.
Standard English grammar and sentence structure are used appropriately for this grade level.	Standard English grammar and sentence structure are used appropriately for this grade level throughout the story.	Standard English grammar and sentence structure are used appropriately for this grade level, with few problems.	Inconsistent use of standard English grammar and sentence structure disrupts readers' comprehension.	Minimal use of standard English grammar and sentence structure confuses readers.

for **WRITING WORKSHOP** *page 222*

Writing: Problem-Solution Essay

Use the chart below (and the rubric on page 32) to evaluate a problem-solution essay. Circle the numbers that best indicate how well the criteria are met. With ten criteria, the lowest possible score is 0, the highest 40.

4 = Clearly meets this criterion

3 = Makes a serious effort to meet this criterion and is fairly successful

2 = Makes some effort to meet this criterion but with little success

1 = Does not achieve this criterion

0 = Unscorable

CRITERIA FOR EVALUATION	RATING
Genre, Organization, and Focus	
Beginning grabs the reader's attention.	4 3 2 1 0
Introduction states the problem.	4 3 2 1 0
Details describe the problem.	4 3 2 1 0
Essay proposes solution to the problem.	4 3 2 1 0
Pros and cons of solution are examined.	4 3 2 1 0
Essay targets audience.	4 3 2 1 0
Paragraphs are in order of importance.	4 3 2 1 0
Conclusion includes call to action.	4 3 2 1 0
Writing Conventions	
Standard English spelling, punctuation, capitalization, and manuscript form are used appropriately for this grade level.	4 3 2 1 0
Standard English grammar and sentence structure are used appropriately for this grade level.	4 3 2 1 0
Total Points:	

Writing: Problem-Solution Essay

CRITERIA FOR EVALUATION	SCORE POINT 4	SCORE POINT 3	SCORE POINT 2	SCORE POINT 1
Genre, Organization, and Focus				
Beginning grabs the reader's attention.	Beginning grabs the reader's attention with a strong statement, a statistic, or a vivid example of the problem.	Beginning only partially develops attention-grabbing opener.	Beginning does not grab the reader's attention but is related to the topic.	Beginning does not grab the reader's attention and is not related to the topic.
Introduction states the problem.	Introduction clearly states the specific problem.	Introduction states the problem but is somewhat general.	Introduction refers to the problem but is unclear.	Introduction is missing or does not mention the problem.
Details describe the problem.	Well-chosen details and examples clearly show the causes, effects, and seriousness of the problem.	Details and examples usually show the causes, effects, and seriousness of the problem.	Details occasionally show the causes or effects but do not establish the seriousness of the problem.	Details are missing or do not show causes, effects, or seriousness of the problem.
Essay proposes solution to the problem.	Essay proposes a clear, reasonable solution to the problem.	Essay proposes a solution to the problem, but solution may be unclear or unrealistic.	Essay mentions a solution to the problem but does not develop it.	Essay omits solution to the problem.
Pros and cons of solution are examined.	Pros and cons of solution are clearly described, and possible objections are addressed.	At least one pro and one con of solution are described, and at least one possible objection is addressed.	At least one pro is described, and one possible objection is mentioned.	No pros or cons of solution are mentioned.
Essay targets audience.	Essay targets appropriate audience with a tone that will reach that audience.	Essay targets appropriate audience, but sometimes the tone is inconsistent.	Essay identifies an audience, but audience or tone is inappropriate.	Essay ignores possible audience.
Paragraphs are in order of importance.	All paragraphs build toward most important idea.	Most paragraphs build toward most important idea.	Paragraphs are generally in an order, but not order of importance.	Paragraphs are in random order, or body of essay is one paragraph.
Conclusion includes call to action.	Conclusion includes a clear, reasonable, convincing call to action.	Conclusion includes a somewhat unclear call to action.	Conclusion includes a general statement of what readers might do but no call to action.	Conclusion does not mention what readers might do, or essay ends abruptly.

CRITERIA FOR EVALUATION	SCORE POINT 4	SCORE POINT 3	SCORE POINT 2	SCORE POINT 1
Writing Conventions				
Standard English spelling, punctuation, capitalization, and manuscript form are used appropriately for this grade level.	Standard English spelling, punctuation, capitalization, and manuscript form are used appropriately for this grade level throughout the essay.	Standard English spelling, punctuation, capitalization, and manuscript form are used appropriately for this grade level, with few problems.	Inconsistent use of standard English spelling, punctuation, capitalization, and manuscript form disrupts readers' comprehension.	Minimal use of standard English spelling, punctuation, capitalization, and manuscript form confuses readers.
Standard English grammar and sentence structure are used appropriately for this grade level.	Standard English grammar and sentence structure are used appropriately for this grade level throughout the essay.	Standard English grammar and sentence structure are used appropriately for this grade level, with few problems.	Inconsistent use of standard English grammar and sentence structure disrupts readers' comprehension.	Minimal use of standard English grammar and sentence structure confuses readers.

SCALES AND RUBRICS

for **WRITING WORKSHOP**   *page 330*   **ANALYTICAL SCALE**

Writing: Personal Narrative

Use the chart below (and the rubric on page 35) to evaluate a personal narrative. Circle the numbers that best indicate how well the criteria are met. With ten criteria, the lowest possible score is 0, the highest 40.

4 = Clearly meets this criterion

3 = Makes a serious effort to meet this criterion and is fairly successful

2 = Makes some effort to meet this criterion but with little success

1 = Does not achieve this criterion

0 = Unscorable

CRITERIA FOR EVALUATION	RATING
Genre, Organization, and Focus	
Introduction grabs the reader's attention.	4 3 2 1 0
Details in introduction set the scene.	4 3 2 1 0
First-person point of view is consistent throughout the narrative.	4 3 2 1 0
Events are in chronological order.	4 3 2 1 0
Transitional words link events.	4 3 2 1 0
Details elaborate upon each event, making people, places, and events seem real.	4 3 2 1 0
Writer's thoughts and feelings are included.	4 3 2 1 0
Conclusion states why the experience is meaningful.	4 3 2 1 0
Writing Conventions	
Standard English spelling, punctuation, capitalization, and manuscript form are used appropriately for this grade level.	4 3 2 1 0
Standard English grammar and sentence structure are used appropriately for this grade level.	4 3 2 1 0
Total Points:	

SCALES AND RUBRICS

Writing: Personal Narrative

CRITERIA FOR EVALUATION	SCORE POINT 4	SCORE POINT 3	SCORE POINT 2	SCORE POINT 1
Genre, Organization, and Focus				
Introduction grabs the reader's attention.	Introduction grabs the reader's attention with a catchy quotation or statement.	Introduction only partially develops the attention-grabbing opener.	Beginning fails to grab the reader's attention, but it is related to the narrative.	Beginning fails to grab the reader's attention and is not related to the narrative.
Details in introduction set the scene.	Specific details in introduction set the scene, creating a vivid picture of when and where the experience happened.	Details in introduction set the scene but are somewhat general.	A few details in introduction partially set the scene, telling only where or when the experience happened.	Introduction does not set the scene.
First-person point of view is consistent throughout the narrative.	First-person point of view is clear and consistent throughout the narrative.	First-person point of view is almost always consistent in the narrative.	A few noticeable shifts from first-person point of view occur.	Point of view is not clear, or it frequently shifts, confusing the reader.
Events are in chronological order.	All events are clearly in chronological order.	Most events are in chronological order.	Some events are in chronological order.	Events are in random order.
Transitional words link events.	Well-chosen transitional words link events, clearly showing their order throughout the narrative.	Transitional words often link events, showing their order in most parts of the narrative.	Transitional words seldom link events, or some transitions are inappropriate.	Transitional words are not used.
Details elaborate upon each event, making people, places, and events seem real.	Relevant details, including sensory details and dialogue, elaborate upon each event, making people, places, and events seem real.	Details, including sensory details and dialogue, elaborate upon most events, usually making people, places, and events seem real.	Details elaborate upon few events, only occasionally making people, places, or events seem real.	Details are omitted.
Writer's thoughts and feelings are included.	Writer's thoughts and feelings are clearly included and related to the narrative.	Writer's thoughts and feelings are included but are not always clearly related to events.	Writer's thoughts and feelings are mentioned but not explained.	Writer's thoughts and feelings are not included in the narrative.

CRITERIA FOR EVALUATION	SCORE POINT 4	SCORE POINT 3	SCORE POINT 2	SCORE POINT 1
Conclusion states why the experience is meaningful.	Conclusion clearly states why the experience is meaningful, including how it changed the writer or what it taught the writer.	Conclusion states why the experience is meaningful, but the connection between the experience and the stated reason is somewhat general.	Conclusion mentions why the experience is meaningful, but the connection to the events is not clear to reader.	Conclusion does not mention why the experience is meaningful.
Writing Conventions				
Standard English spelling, punctuation, capitalization, and manuscript form are used appropriately for this grade level.	Standard English spelling, punctuation, capitalization, and manuscript form are used appropriately for this grade level throughout the narrative.	Standard English spelling, punctuation, capitalization, and manuscript form are used appropriately for this grade level, with few problems.	Inconsistent use of standard English spelling, punctuation, capitalization, and manuscript form disrupts readers' comprehension.	Minimal use of standard English spelling, punctuation, capitalization, and manuscript form confuses readers.
Standard English grammar and sentence structure are used appropriately for this grade level.	Standard English grammar and sentence structure are used appropriately for this grade level throughout the narrative.	Standard English grammar and sentence structure are used appropriately for this grade level, with few problems.	Inconsistent use of standard English grammar and sentence structure disrupts readers' comprehension.	Minimal use of standard English grammar and sentence structure confuses readers.

Writing: Descriptive Essay

Use the chart below (and the rubric on page 38) to evaluate a descriptive essay. Circle the numbers that best indicate how well the criteria are met. With eight criteria, the lowest possible score is 0, the highest 32.

4 = Clearly meets this criterion

3 = Makes a serious effort to meet this criterion and is fairly successful

2 = Makes some effort to meet this criterion but with little success

1 = Does not achieve this criterion

0 = Unscorable

CRITERIA FOR EVALUATION	RATING
Genre, Organization, and Focus	
Introduction identifies the subject, the time, and the place and provides background information.	4 3 2 1 0
Precise words and figures of speech bring sensory details to life.	4 3 2 1 0
Details are arranged in a clear, logical order.	4 3 2 1 0
Transitions link ideas.	4 3 2 1 0
Writer's thoughts and feelings about the subject are included.	4 3 2 1 0
Conclusion states why the subject is significant and conveys overall impression.	4 3 2 1 0
Writing Conventions	
Standard English spelling, punctuation, capitalization, and manuscript form are used appropriately for this grade level.	4 3 2 1 0
Standard English grammar and sentence structure are used appropriately for this grade level.	4 3 2 1 0
Total Points:	

Writing: Descriptive Essay

▶ **Genre, Organization, and Focus**

CRITERIA FOR EVALUATION	SCORE POINT 4	SCORE POINT 3	SCORE POINT 2	SCORE POINT 1
Introduction identifies the subject, the time, and the place and provides background information.	Introduction clearly identifies the subject, the time, and the place and provides necessary background information.	Introduction identifies the subject, the time, and the place and provides some background information, but some details are unclear.	Introduction refers to the subject, but the time or place is unclear, and necessary background information is missing.	Introduction does not identify the subject.
Precise words and figures of speech bring sensory details to life.	Precise words and figures of speech consistently bring sensory details to life.	Precise words and figures of speech often enhance the description of sensory details.	Precise words and figures of speech are seldom used.	Vague words make the ideas unclear.
Details are arranged in a clear, logical order.	All details are logically arranged, by spatial order, order of importance, or chronological order.	Details are arranged by spatial order, order of importance, or chronological order, with only minor lapses.	Arrangement of details is not logical; few details are in spatial order, order of importance, or chronological order.	Details are in random order and are confusing to reader.
Transitions link ideas.	Effective transitions clearly link ideas throughout the essay.	Effective transitions often link ideas.	Few transitions are used, or some transitions are inappropriate.	Transitions are missing or inappropriate.
Writer's thoughts and feelings about the subject are included.	Specific details about writer's thoughts and feelings about the subject are clearly and appropriately expressed.	Several details about the writer's thoughts and feelings are included.	Few details about the writer's thoughts and feelings are included, making the essay feel impersonal.	Writer's thoughts and feelings are not included in the essay.
Conclusion states why the subject is significant and conveys overall impression.	Conclusion clearly states why the subject is significant and conveys overall impression.	Conclusion contributes to overall impression of essay, but why the subject is significant is unclear.	Conclusion omits statement about significance of subject or does not sustain overall impression.	Conclusion omits statement about significance of subject and does not contribute to overall impression.

CRITERIA FOR EVALUATION	SCORE POINT 4	SCORE POINT 3	SCORE POINT 2	SCORE POINT 1
Writing Conventions				
Standard English spelling, punctuation, capitalization, and manuscript form are used appropriately for this grade level.	Standard English spelling, punctuation, capitalization, and manuscript form are used appropriately for this grade level throughout the essay.	Standard English spelling, punctuation, capitalization, and manuscript form are used appropriately for this grade level, with few problems.	Inconsistent use of standard English spelling, punctuation, capitalization, and manuscript form disrupts readers' comprehension.	Minimal use of standard English spelling, punctuation, capitalization, and manuscript form confuses readers.
Standard English grammar and sentence structure are used appropriately for this grade level.	Standard English grammar and sentence structure are used appropriately for this grade level throughout the essay.	Standard English grammar and sentence structure are used appropriately for this grade level, with few problems.	Inconsistent use of standard English grammar and sentence structure disrupts readers' comprehension.	Minimal use of standard English grammar and sentence structure confuses readers.

SCALES AND RUBRICS

Writing: Supporting an Interpretation

Use the chart below (and the rubric on page 41) to evaluate an interpretation of a literary work. Circle the numbers that best indicate how well the criteria are met. With these eight criteria, the lowest possible score is 0, the highest 32.

4 = Clearly meets this criterion

3 = Makes a serious effort to meet this criterion and is fairly successful

2 = Makes some effort to meet this criterion but with little success

1 = Does not achieve this criterion

0 = Unscorable

CRITERIA FOR EVALUATION	RATING
Genre, Organization, and Focus	
Introduction names the author and title.	4 3 2 1 0
Introduction includes a clear thesis.	4 3 2 1 0
Main idea of each body paragraph is clear and supports the thesis.	4 3 2 1 0
Evidence supports the main idea of each body paragraph.	4 3 2 1 0
Conclusion restates the thesis and summarizes the main points.	4 3 2 1 0
Conclusion leaves readers with something to consider.	4 3 2 1 0
Writing Conventions	
Standard English spelling, punctuation, capitalization, and manuscript form are used appropriately for this grade level.	4 3 2 1 0
Standard English grammar and sentence structure are used appropriately for this grade level.	4 3 2 1 0
Total Points:	

Writing: Supporting an Interpretation

CRITERIA FOR EVALUATION	SCORE POINT 4	SCORE POINT 3	SCORE POINT 2	SCORE POINT 1
Genre, Organization, and Focus				
Introduction names the author and title.	Introduction accurately and completely names the author and title.	Introduction accurately names the author and title, but some information is general or incomplete.	Introduction omits the name of the author or title, or some information is not correct.	Introduction does not name the author or title.
Introduction includes a clear thesis.	Introduction includes a clear, specific thesis.	Introduction includes a fairly clear thesis statement.	Introduction includes a general statement of what the essay is about.	Introduction includes no statement of what the essay is about.
Main idea of each body paragraph is clear and supports the thesis.	Main idea of each body paragraph is clear and effectively supports the thesis.	Main idea of each body paragraph is fairly clear and generally supports the thesis.	Main idea of each body paragraph is not always clear or does not support the thesis.	All main ideas are discussed in only one paragraph, or main ideas do not support the thesis.
Evidence supports the main idea of each body paragraph.	Well-chosen evidence (details and quotations) clearly supports the main idea of each body paragraph.	Evidence (details and quotations) usually supports the main idea of each body paragraph.	Evidence (details and quotations) only occasionally supports the main ideas.	Evidence to support the main ideas is missing.
Conclusion restates the thesis and summarizes the main points.	Conclusion clearly and effectively restates the thesis and summarizes all main points.	Conclusion generally restates the thesis and summarizes most main points.	Conclusion only hints at the thesis or simply repeats the thesis statement from the introduction.	Conclusion lacks any restatement of the thesis.
Conclusion leaves readers with something to consider.	Conclusion leaves readers with something to consider by perceptively applying the thesis to a broader experience or connecting it with other works.	Conclusion leaves readers with something to consider by stating some connection to a broader experience or to other works.	Conclusion includes a statement about some lesson to be learned, but the statement is unclear or not related to the analysis.	Conclusion lacks any statement of something for readers to consider.

SCALES AND RUBRICS

SCALES AND RUBRICS

CRITERIA FOR EVALUATION	SCORE POINT 4	SCORE POINT 3	SCORE POINT 2	SCORE POINT 1
Writing Conventions				
Standard English spelling, punctuation, capitalization, and manuscript form are used appropriately for this grade level.	Standard English spelling, punctuation, capitalization, and manuscript form are used appropriately for this grade level throughout the essay.	Standard English spelling, punctuation, capitalization, and manuscript form are used appropriately for this grade level, with few problems.	Inconsistent use of standard English spelling, punctuation, capitalization, and manuscript form disrupts readers' comprehension.	Minimal use of standard English spelling, punctuation, capitalization, and manuscript form confuses readers.
Standard English grammar and sentence structure are used appropriately for this grade level.	Standard English grammar and sentence structure are used appropriately for this grade level throughout the essay.	Standard English grammar and sentence structure are used appropriately for this grade level, with few problems.	Inconsistent use of standard English grammar and sentence structure disrupts readers' comprehension.	Minimal use of standard English grammar and sentence structure confuses readers.

ANALYTICAL SCALE

Writing: Comparison-Contrast Essay

Use the chart below (and the rubric on page 44) to evaluate a comparison-contrast essay. Circle the numbers that best indicate how well the criteria are met. With these eight criteria, the lowest possible score is 0, the highest 32.

4 = Clearly meets this criterion

3 = Makes a serious effort to meet this criterion and is fairly successful

2 = Makes some effort to meet this criterion but with little success

1 = Does not achieve this criterion

0 = Unscorable

CRITERIA FOR EVALUATION	RATING
Genre, Organization, and Focus	
Introduction states the thesis and identifies literary works by title and author's name.	4 3 2 1 0
Essay discusses two or more similarities or differences.	4 3 2 1 0
Organization follows either block or point-by-point method.	4 3 2 1 0
Transitional words and phrases show comparison or contrast.	4 3 2 1 0
Details and examples support general statements.	4 3 2 1 0
Conclusion restates and expands on the main idea.	4 3 2 1 0
Writing Conventions	
Standard English spelling, punctuation, capitalization, and manuscript form are used appropriately for this grade level.	4 3 2 1 0
Standard English grammar and sentence structure are used appropriately for this grade level.	4 3 2 1 0
Total Points:	

SCALES AND RUBRICS

Writing: Comparison-Contrast Essay

CRITERIA FOR EVALUATION	SCORE POINT 4	SCORE POINT 3	SCORE POINT 2	SCORE POINT 1
Genre, Organization, and Focus				
Introduction states the thesis and identifies literary works by title and author's name.	Introduction clearly states the thesis and accurately identifies literary works by title and author's name.	Introduction generally indicates the thesis but incompletely identifies literary works.	Introduction omits a thesis statement or does not identify one of the literary works.	Introduction omits a thesis statement and does not identify the literary works.
Essay discusses two or more similarities or differences.	Essay clearly discusses two or more significant similarities or differences.	Essay discusses two similarities or differences, but one is not significant.	Essay discusses only one similarity or difference.	Essay does not compare or contrast the two works or discusses only one literary work.
Organization follows either block or point-by-point method.	Organization clearly and logically follows either block or point-by-point method.	Organization generally follows either block or point-by-point method, with few lapses.	Some sections of essay are organized point by point, but organization is inconsistent and sometimes difficult to follow.	Essay is disorganized, with points of comparison in no clear order.
Transitional words and phrases show comparison or contrast.	Well-chosen transitional words and phrases clearly show comparison or contrast.	Some appropriate transitional words and phrases help the reader identify points of comparison or contrast.	Few transitional words and phrases are used.	Transitional words are missing or inappropriate.
Details and examples support general statements.	Appropriate details and examples support every general statement.	Details and examples support most general statements.	General statements are often unsupported, or some details and examples are inappropriate.	Details and examples are missing.
Conclusion restates and expands on the main idea.	Conclusion clearly restates and appropriately expands on the main idea.	Conclusion restates but does not expand on the main idea.	Conclusion repeats the statement of the main idea from the introduction.	Essay ends abruptly, or conclusion lacks a restatement of the main idea.

CRITERIA FOR EVALUATION	SCORE POINT 4	SCORE POINT 3	SCORE POINT 2	SCORE POINT 1
Writing Conventions				
Standard English spelling, punctuation, capitalization, and manuscript form are used appropriately for this grade level.	Standard English spelling, punctuation, capitalization, and manuscript form are used appropriately for this grade level throughout the essay.	Standard English spelling, punctuation, capitalization, and manuscript form are used appropriately for this grade level, with few problems.	Inconsistent use of standard English spelling, punctuation, capitalization, and manuscript form disrupts readers' comprehension.	Minimal use of standard English spelling, punctuation, capitalization, and manuscript form confuses readers.
Standard English grammar and sentence structure are used appropriately for this grade level.	Standard English grammar and sentence structure are used appropriately for this grade level throughout the essay.	Standard English grammar and sentence structure are used appropriately for this grade level, with few problems.	Inconsistent use of standard English grammar and sentence structure disrupts readers' comprehension.	Minimal use of standard English grammar and sentence structure confuses readers.

for **WRITING WORKSHOP** *page 864*   **ANALYTICAL SCALE**

Writing: Informative Report

Use the chart below (and the rubric on page 47) to evaluate an informative report. Circle the numbers that best indicate how well the criteria are met. With these eight criteria, the lowest possible score is 0, the highest 32.

4 = Clearly meets this criterion

3 = Makes a serious effort to meet this criterion and is fairly successful

2 = Makes some effort to meet this criterion but with little success

1 = Does not achieve this criterion

0 = Unscorable

CRITERIA FOR EVALUATION	RATING
Genre, Organization, and Focus	
Thesis statement identifies the report's topic and the main idea.	4 3 2 1 0
Each body paragraph develops only one subtopic.	4 3 2 1 0
Supporting evidence elaborates upon each subtopic.	4 3 2 1 0
Transitional words and phrases link ideas.	4 3 2 1 0
Conclusion sums up the overall findings.	4 3 2 1 0
Sources in the Works Cited list are accurately documented and in alphabetical order.	4 3 2 1 0
Writing Conventions	
Standard English spelling, punctuation, capitalization, and manuscript form are used appropriately for this grade level.	4 3 2 1 0
Standard English grammar and sentence structure are used appropriately for this grade level.	4 3 2 1 0
Total Points:	

SCALES AND RUBRICS

Writing: Informative Report

CRITERIA FOR EVALUATION	SCORE POINT 4	SCORE POINT 3	SCORE POINT 2	SCORE POINT 1
Genre, Organization, and Focus				
Thesis statement identifies the report's topic and the main idea.	Thesis statement clearly identifies the report's topic and the main idea about the topic.	Thesis statement identifies the report's topic but not the main idea about the topic.	Thesis statement is incomplete or confusing and unclear.	Introduction omits thesis statement.
Each body paragraph develops only one subtopic.	Each body paragraph distinctly develops only one subtopic.	Most body paragraphs develop only one subtopic each, but occasionally more than one subtopic appears in a single paragraph.	Body paragraphs often contain more than one subtopic.	Body paragraphs fragment subtopics into several miniature paragraphs, or entire body is only one or two paragraphs.
Supporting evidence elaborates upon each subtopic.	Supporting evidence (facts, examples, and direct quotations) clearly and appropriately elaborates upon each subtopic.	Supporting evidence (facts, examples, and direct quotations) clearly elaborates upon most subtopics.	Supporting evidence elaborates upon a few of the subtopics, but the connection between some evidence and the subtopics may be unclear.	The subtopics are largely unsupported by evidence.
Transitional words and phrases link ideas.	Carefully chosen transitional words and phrases link ideas.	Several appropriate transitional words and phrases link some ideas.	Few transitional words and phrases are used.	Transitional words are missing or inappropriate.
Conclusion sums up the overall findings.	Conclusion clearly and concisely sums up overall findings about the topic.	Conclusion sums up some of the findings about the topic.	Conclusion repeats thesis statement from the introduction or sums up one or two subtopics.	Conclusion does not sum up findings.
Sources in Works Cited list are accurately documented and in alphabetical order.	All sources in Works Cited list are accurately documented and in alphabetical order.	Most sources in Works Cited list are accurately documented and in alphabetical order, but some identifying information is missing.	Only two sources are listed in Works Cited list, or major identifying information is missing or inaccurate.	Works Cited list is missing.

CRITERIA FOR EVALUATION	SCORE POINT 4	SCORE POINT 3	SCORE POINT 2	SCORE POINT 1
Writing Conventions				
Standard English spelling, punctuation, capitalization, and manuscript form are used appropriately for this grade level.	Standard English spelling, punctuation, capitalization, and manuscript form are used appropriately for this grade level throughout the report.	Standard English spelling, punctuation, capitalization, and manuscript form are used appropriately for this grade level, with few problems.	Inconsistent use of standard English spelling, punctuation, capitalization, and manuscript form disrupts readers' comprehension.	Minimal use of standard English spelling, punctuation, capitalization, and manuscript form confuses readers.
Standard English grammar and sentence structure are used appropriately for this grade level.	Standard English grammar and sentence structure are used appropriately for this grade level throughout the report.	Standard English grammar and sentence structure are used appropriately for this grade level, with few problems.	Inconsistent use of standard English grammar and sentence structure disrupts readers' comprehension.	Minimal use of standard English grammar and sentence structure confuses readers.

Multimedia Presentation: Public-Service Announcement

Use the chart below (and the rubric on page 50) to evaluate a public-service announcement. Circle the numbers that best indicate how well the criteria are met. With these six criteria, the lowest possible score is 0, the highest 24.

4 = Clearly meets this criterion

3 = Makes a serious effort to meet this criterion and is fairly successful

2 = Makes some effort to meet this criterion but with little success

1 = Does not achieve this criterion

0 = Unscorable

CRITERIA FOR EVALUATION	RATING
Content, Organization, and Focus	
Introduction states the purpose of the message.	4 3 2 1 0
Announcement targets the audience for the message.	4 3 2 1 0
Facts, examples, and other evidence support the message.	4 3 2 1 0
Presentation includes different forms of media.	4 3 2 1 0
Conclusion wraps up the message.	4 3 2 1 0
Language Conventions	
Standard English grammar and sentence structure are used appropriately for this grade level.	4 3 2 1 0
Total Points:	

Multimedia Presentation: Public-Service Announcement

CRITERIA FOR EVALUATION	SCORE POINT 4	SCORE POINT 3	SCORE POINT 2	SCORE POINT 1
Genre, Organization, and Focus				
Introduction states the purpose of the message.	Introduction clearly states the purpose of the message, showing its importance.	Introduction generally states the purpose of the message and its importance.	Introduction refers to the purpose of the message, but its importance is unclear.	Introduction does not mention the purpose of the message.
Announcement targets the audience for the message.	Announcement clearly identifies and targets the audience affected by the message.	Announcement targets an audience affected by the message but does not tailor all parts of the message to that audience.	Announcement targets an audience, but not one clearly affected by the message.	Announcement ignores audience.
Facts, examples, and other evidence support the message.	Clear, appropriate facts, examples, and other evidence support all main points of the message.	Appropriate facts, examples, and other evidence support most of the main points of the message.	Facts, examples, and other evidence support a few of the main points, but some necessary evidence is missing.	Facts, examples, and other evidence are not provided, or they are not appropriate.
Presentation includes different forms of media.	Presentation includes different forms of media that effectively support the message.	Presentation includes two different forms of media that generally support the message.	Presentation includes one form of media, but its connection to the message may be unclear.	No media are used, or the media are not related to the message.
Conclusion wraps up the message.	Conclusion wraps up the message with a clear restatement of the presenter's position or a dramatic quotation.	Conclusion wraps up the message with a general restatement of the presenter's position.	Conclusion repeats the statement of the purpose from the introduction.	Conclusion omits a restatement of the presenter's position.

CRITERIA FOR EVALUATION	SCORE POINT 4	SCORE POINT 3	SCORE POINT 2	SCORE POINT 1
Language Conventions				
Standard English grammar and sentence structure are used appropriately for this grade level.	Standard English grammar and sentence structure are used appropriately for this grade level throughout the presentation.	Standard English grammar and sentence structure are used appropriately for this grade level, with few problems.	Inconsistent use of standard English grammar and sentence structure disrupts the audience's comprehension.	Minimal use of standard English grammar and sentence structure confuses the audience.

Personal Narrative

Use the chart below (and the rubric on page 53) to score an oral narrative and its evaluation. Circle the numbers that best indicate how well the criteria are met. With these seven criteria, the lowest possible score is 0, the highest 28.

4 = Clearly meets this criterion

3 = Makes a serious effort to meet this criterion and is fairly successful

2 = Makes some effort to meet this criterion but with little success

1 = Does not achieve this criterion

0 = Unscorable

CRITERIA FOR EVALUATION	RATING
Genre and Organization	
Story appeals to the audience.	4 3 2 1 0
Plot is organized logically and builds suspense.	4 3 2 1 0
Point of view is consistent.	4 3 2 1 0
Vivid language and specific details describe the setting and bring the characters to life.	4 3 2 1 0
Delivery and Comprehension	
Speaking techniques emphasize important moments and make the story come alive.	4 3 2 1 0
Listener evaluates content, delivery, and overall impact of the presentation and offers feedback.	4 3 2 1 0
Oral Language Conventions	
Standard English is used appropriately for this grade level except in specific, realistic dialogue important to the narrative.	4 3 2 1 0
Total Points:	

SCALES AND RUBRICS

Personal Narrative

CRITERIA FOR EVALUATION	SCORE POINT 4	SCORE POINT 3	SCORE POINT 2	SCORE POINT 1
Genre, Organization, and Focus				
Story appeals to the audience.	Story clearly appeals to the backgrounds and interests of the audience.	Story generally appeals to the backgrounds and interests of the audience.	Story does not give the audience details necessary for appealing to their backgrounds and interests.	Story is dull and uninteresting.
Plot is organized logically and builds suspense.	Plot is organized logically for the particular audience and builds suspense effectively.	Plot is generally organized logically, and suspense is only partly developed.	Plot is not organized consistently, and the resolution is given away early in the narrative.	Plot events are narrated in random order, confusing the audience.
Point of view is consistent.	Point of view is consistent throughout the story.	Point of view is usually consistent, with only one or two shifts.	Point of view shifts several times.	Point of view is inconsistent and confusing.
Vivid language and specific details describe the setting and bring the characters to life.	Vivid language and specific details describe the setting and bring the characters to life throughout the narrative.	Vivid language and specific details describe the setting and the characters in most parts of the narrative.	Setting and characters are only occasionally described with vivid language or specific details.	Lack of vivid language and specific details prevents listeners from picturing the setting or the characters.
Delivery and Comprehension				
Speaking techniques emphasize important moments and make the story come alive.	Effective speaking techniques (facial expressions, gestures, movements, voice modulation, inflection, tempo, enunciation, eye contact) emphasize important moments and make the entire story come alive.	Speaking techniques emphasize most important moments and usually make the story come alive.	Speaking techniques emphasize some important moments, but sometimes they are used inappropriately, distracting the audience.	Speaking techniques do not emphasize important moments; if used, they confuse the audience or are not effective.

SCALES AND RUBRICS

CRITERIA FOR EVALUATION	SCORE POINT 4	SCORE POINT 3	SCORE POINT 2	SCORE POINT 1
Listener evaluates content, delivery, and overall impact of the presentation and offers feedback.	Listener accurately and thoroughly evaluates content, delivery, and overall impact of the presentation and offers appropriate, constructive feedback.	Listener accurately evaluates most content and some delivery techniques of the presentation and offers some appropriate feedback.	Listener summarizes some content and identifies at least one verbal and one nonverbal speaking technique used in the presentation, but feedback is superficial.	Listener mentions a few details from the presentation but omits speaking techniques and offers no appropriate feedback.
Oral Language Conventions				
Standard English is used appropriately for this grade level except in specific, realistic dialogue important to the narrative.	Standard English appropriate to this grade level is used consistently throughout the narrative, except in specific, realistic dialogue important to the narrative.	Standard English is used appropriately for this grade level, with few problems.	Inconsistent use of standard English jars the listener.	Minimal use of standard English confuses the listener.

for **SPEAKING AND LISTENING**   *page 1050*   **ANALYTICAL SCALE**

Persuasive Speech

Use the chart below (and the rubric on page 56) to score a persuasive speech and its evaluation. Circle the numbers that best indicate how well the criteria are met. With these seven criteria, the lowest possible score is 0, the highest 28.

4 = Clearly meets this criterion

3 = Makes a serious effort to meet this criterion and is fairly successful

2 = Makes some effort to meet this criterion but with little success

1 = Does not achieve this criterion

0 = Unscorable

CRITERIA FOR EVALUATION	RATING
Genre, Organization, and Focus	
Background information presented is appropriate for the particular audience.	4 3 2 1 0
Ideas are organized persuasively for the particular audience.	4 3 2 1 0
Reasons and evidence related to the background and interests of the audience support the opinion.	4 3 2 1 0
Delivery and Comprehension	
Speaking techniques emphasize important points and hold the audience's attention.	4 3 2 1 0
Listener evaluates content, believability, and delivery techniques of speech.	4 3 2 1 0
Listener gives appropriate feedback to speaker.	4 3 2 1 0
Oral Language Conventions	
Standard English is used appropriately for this grade level.	4 3 2 1 0
Total Points:	

SCALES AND RUBRICS

Persuasive Speech

CRITERIA FOR EVALUATION	SCORE POINT 4	SCORE POINT 3	SCORE POINT 2	SCORE POINT 1
Genre, Organization, and Focus				
Background information presented is appropriate for the particular audience.	Background information presented is thorough and appropriate for the particular audience.	Most background information presented is appropriate for the particular audience, but more information is needed.	Few background details appropriate for the particular audience are presented, and information is insufficient to prepare audience for the speech.	No background information appropriate for the particular audience is presented.
Ideas are organized persuasively for the particular audience.	Ideas are organized clearly and persuasively, considering the background and interests of the particular audience.	Ideas are organized with the audience in mind, but sometimes organization is not clear.	Organization is not tailored to appeal to the audience.	Speech demonstrates no organizational frame or attempt to tailor the speech to the particular audience.
Reasons and evidence related to the background and interests of the audience support the opinion.	Reasons and evidence (examples, anecdotes, facts, statistics, expert opinions) clearly related to the background and interests of the audience persuasively support the opinion.	Reasons and evidence somewhat related to the background and interests of the audience support the opinion.	At least one reason and some evidence support the opinion, but the evidence is not related to the background and interests of the audience.	No reasons or evidence supports the opinion.
Delivery and Comprehension				
Speaking techniques emphasize important points and hold the audience's attention.	Skillfully used speaking techniques (enunciation, vocal modulation, inflection, tempo, eye contact) emphasize all important points and hold the audience's attention throughout the speech.	Appropriate speaking techniques (enunciation, vocal modulation, inflection, tempo, eye contact) emphasize most important points and usually hold the audience's attention.	Speaking techniques (enunciation, vocal modulation, inflection, tempo, eye contact) occasionally emphasize important points but are sometimes used inappropriately, distracting the audience from the message.	Speech is delivered in a monotone, or speaking techniques are used so inappropriately that they confuse the audience.

CRITERIA FOR EVALUATION	SCORE POINT 4	SCORE POINT 3	SCORE POINT 2	SCORE POINT 1
Listener evaluates content, believability, and delivery techniques of speech.	Listener thoroughly evaluates content of speech, including supporting evidence and organization, believability, and delivery techniques.	Listener evaluates content of speech, believability, and delivery techniques, with few omissions.	Listener summarizes content, mentions believability, and identifies at least two delivery techniques, but evaluation is superficial or unclear.	Listener does not evaluate speech, but merely lists content.
Listener gives appropriate feedback to speaker.	Listener gives clear, thoughtful, thorough feedback, including questions to get more information or clarify points, to speaker.	Listener gives mostly appropriate feedback to speaker, or feedback is somewhat vague.	Listener gives at least one appropriate, though vague, feedback comment.	Listener gives no appropriate feedback; any comments at end of speech are irrelevant to the topic and delivery.

Oral Language Conventions

Standard English is used appropriately for this grade level.	Standard English is used appropriately for this grade level throughout the speech and/or evaluation.	Standard English is used appropriately for this grade level, with few problems.	Inconsistent use of standard English jars the listener.	Minimal use of standard English confuses the listener.

SCALES AND RUBRICS

Informative Speech

Use the chart below (and the rubric on page 59) to score an informative speech and its evaluation. Circle the numbers that best indicate how well the criteria and standards are met. With these ten criteria, the lowest possible score is 0, the highest 40.

4 = Clearly meets this criterion

3 = Makes a serious effort to meet this criterion and is fairly successful

2 = Makes some effort to meet this criterion but with little success

1 = Does not achieve this criterion

0 = Unscorable

CRITERIA FOR EVALUATION	RATING
Genre, Organization, and Focus	
Opening catches listeners' interest.	4 3 2 1 0
Thesis statement presents a focused topic and purpose.	4 3 2 1 0
Organization helps audience understand the main ideas.	4 3 2 1 0
Support from sources includes a variety of perspectives on the topic.	4 3 2 1 0
Sources are credited.	4 3 2 1 0
Any audiovisual materials used make ideas clear.	4 3 2 1 0
Conclusion re-emphasizes main idea of speech.	4 3 2 1 0
Delivery and Comprehension	
Speaking techniques help the audience understand the information.	4 3 2 1 0
Listener analyzes content, organization, and delivery techniques and provides constructive feedback to speaker.	4 3 2 1 0
Oral Language Conventions	
Standard English is used appropriately for this grade level.	4 3 2 1 0
Total Points:	

Informative Speech

CRITERIA FOR EVALUATION	SCORE POINT 4	SCORE POINT 3	SCORE POINT 2	SCORE POINT 1
Genre, Organization, and Focus				
Opening catches listeners' interest.	Opening catches listeners' interest with a question, an anecdote, or a startling fact.	Opening catches interest of some listeners but is only partially developed.	Opening attempts to appeal to listeners but is only minimally successful.	Opening is trite and ignores listeners.
Thesis statement presents a focused topic and purpose.	Thesis statement clearly and thoroughly presents a narrowly focused topic and purpose.	Thesis statement presents a somewhat focused topic and purpose.	Vague thesis statement presents a general topic and purpose.	Thesis statement is missing or irrelevant to topic.
Organization helps audience understand the main ideas.	Effective, logical organization clearly helps audience understand the main ideas.	Organization is mostly tailored to help the particular audience understand the main ideas, but connections between some ideas are not clear.	Organization is inconsistent, but some attempt has been made to help audience understand the main ideas.	Lack of organization confuses the audience.
Support from sources includes a variety of perspectives on the topic.	Support from sources includes a variety of clearly explained perspectives on the topic.	Support from sources includes a variety of perspectives, but all are not clearly explained.	Support includes more than one perspective, but they are poorly explained.	Support represents only one perspective.
Sources are credited.	All sources are clearly credited.	All sources are credited, but some identifying information is omitted.	Some sources are credited but cannot be identified from the information provided.	No sources are credited, or they are credited inaccurately.
Any audiovisual materials used make ideas clear.	Audiovisual materials make ideas clear and are clear and large enough for the audience to see.	Audiovisual materials help make ideas clear and are relatively clear, visible, and appropriate.	Any audiovisual materials used are vague or distracting.	Any audiovisual materials are irrelevant, inaccurate, and/or confusing.
Conclusion re-emphasizes main idea of speech.	Conclusion clearly re-emphasizes main idea of speech by summarizing the most important information in the report or by echoing introduction.	Conclusion generally re-emphasizes main idea of speech by summarizing most major points or echoing introduction.	Conclusion vaguely summarizes a major point or repeats thesis from introduction.	Formal conclusion is missing.

SCALES AND RUBRICS

CRITERIA FOR EVALUATION	SCORE POINT 4	SCORE POINT 3	SCORE POINT 2	SCORE POINT 1
▶ Delivery and Comprehension				
Speaking techniques help the audience understand the information.	Effective speaking techniques help the audience understand all the information presented.	Speaking techniques often help the audience understand the information.	Speaking techniques are only occasionally used appropriately; their inappropriate use sometimes distracts the audience.	Speech is delivered in a monotone, or speaking techniques are used so inappropriately that they confuse the audience.
Listener analyzes content, organization, and delivery techniques and provides constructive feedback to speaker.	Listener perceptively and thoroughly analyzes all elements of content, organization, and delivery techniques and provides insightful, constructive feedback, including probing questions focused on presentation.	Listener analyzes most elements of content, organization, and delivery techniques and provides appropriate feedback, including questions, but feedback is superficial.	Listener vaguely analyzes at least one element of content, organization, and delivery techniques and provides sparse or inappropriate feedback.	Listener merely summarizes some of content, or analysis is inaccurate and feedback is missing, inappropriate, or irrelevant.
▶ Oral Language Conventions				
Standard English is used appropriately for this grade level.	Standard English is used appropriately for this grade level throughout the speech and/or evaluation.	Standard English is used appropriately for this grade level, with few problems.	Inconsistent use of standard English jars the listener.	Minimal use of standard English confuses the reader.

ANALYTICAL SCALE

Poetry Reading

Use the chart below (and the rubric on page 62) to score the recitation of a poem and the evaluation of the recitation. Circle the numbers that best indicate how well the criteria are met. With these seven criteria, the lowest possible score is 0, the highest 28.

4 – Clearly meets this criterion

3 = Makes a serious effort to meet this criterion and is fairly successful

2 = Makes some effort to meet this criterion but with little success

1 = Does not achieve this criterion

0 = Unscorable

CRITERIA FOR EVALUATION	RATING
Delivery	
Reader leaves the audience with an impression of the poem by emphasizing the effects of rhyme, imagery, and language.	4 3 2 1 0
Reader's tone of voice matches the speaker's voice in the poem.	4 3 2 1 0
Reader speaks at a speed that allows the audience to follow the words in the poem.	4 3 2 1 0
Reader stresses appropriate words.	4 3 2 1 0
Reader maintains eye contact with the entire audience.	4 3 2 1 0
Reader speaks loudly and clearly enough for everyone to hear and understand.	4 3 2 1 0
Evaluation	
Listener evaluates the delivery of the recitation.	4 3 2 1 0
Total Points:	

SCALES AND RUBRICS

Poetry Reading

CRITERIA FOR EVALUATION	SCORE POINT 4	SCORE POINT 3	SCORE POINT 2	SCORE POINT 1
Delivery				
Reader leaves the audience with an impression of the poem by emphasizing the effects of rhyme, imagery, and language.	Reader leaves the audience with a clear, accurate impression of the poem by emphasizing the effects of rhyme, imagery, and language.	Reader leaves the audience with a general impression by usually emphasizing the effects of rhyme, imagery, and language.	Reader only occasionally emphasizes the effects of rhyme, imagery, and language.	Reader ignores the effects of rhyme, imagery, and language.
Reader's tone of voice matches the speaker's voice in the poem.	Reader's tone of voice always matches the speaker's voice in the poem.	Reader's tone of voice matches the speaker's voice in the poem during most of the recitation.	Reader's tone of voice sometimes matches the speaker's voice in the poem.	Reader's tone of voice is inappropriate for the poem.
Reader speaks at a speed that allows the audience to follow the words in the poem.	Reader always speaks at a speed that allows the audience to follow the words in the poem.	Reader usually speaks at a speed that allows the audience to follow the words in the poem.	Reader sometimes speeds up or slows down inappropriately, making it difficult for the audience to follow the words in the poem.	Reader's speed is not related to the needs of the audience and often makes it difficult for listeners to understand the poem.
Reader stresses appropriate words.	Reader stresses appropriate words throughout the recitation.	Reader often stresses appropriate words during the recitation.	Reader inappropriately stresses or fails to stress words, marring the recitation.	Reader does not stress any important words in the poem.
Reader maintains eye contact with the entire audience.	Reader maintains eye contact with the entire audience during the recitation.	Reader often maintains eye contact with the audience but sometimes looks down at notes for minutes at a time.	Reader makes eye contact with the audience several times during the recitation.	Reader does not look at the audience during the recitation.
Reader speaks loudly and clearly enough for everyone to hear and understand.	Reader speaks loudly and clearly enough for everyone to hear and understand during the entire recitation.	Reader usually speaks loudly and clearly enough for everyone to hear and understand.	Reader only sometimes speaks loudly and clearly enough for the audience to hear and understand parts of the recitation.	Reader mumbles or speaks so quietly that most listeners cannot hear or understand the recitation.

CRITERIA FOR EVALUATION	SCORE POINT 4	SCORE POINT 3	SCORE POINT 2	SCORE POINT 1
Evaluation				
Listener evaluates the delivery of the recitation.	Listener thoroughly and accurately evaluates all elements of the delivery of the recitation.	Listener evaluates most elements of the delivery of the recitation.	Listener identifies a few elements of the delivery of the recitation but does not adequately evaluate it.	Listener does not identify any elements of the delivery or gives only irrelevant comments.

SCALES AND RUBRICS

Interviewing

Use the chart below (and the rubric on page 65) to score an interview. Circle the numbers that best indicate how well the criteria are met. With these seven criteria, the lowest possible score is 0, the highest 28.

4 = Clearly meets this criterion

3 = Makes a serious effort to meet this criterion and is fairly successful

2 = Makes some effort to meet this criterion but with little success

1 = Does not achieve this criterion

0 = Unscorable

CRITERIA FOR EVALUATION	RATING
Genre and Organization	
Interviewer sets ground rules at the beginning of the interview.	4 3 2 1 0
Interviewer allows the subject to answer questions completely, without interruptions.	4 3 2 1 0
Interviewer asks for explanations and modifies the plan of the interview as appropriate.	4 3 2 1 0
Interviewer keeps the focus on the subject.	4 3 2 1 0
Interviewer courteously wraps up the interview.	4 3 2 1 0
If necessary, interviewer follows up to check facts after the interview.	4 3 2 1 0
Oral Language Conventions	
Standard English is used appropriately for this grade level.	4 3 2 1 0
Total Points:	

SCALES AND RUBRICS

Interviewing

CRITERIA FOR EVALUATION	SCORE POINT 4	SCORE POINT 3	SCORE POINT 2	SCORE POINT 1
Genre and Organization				
Interviewer sets ground rules at the beginning of the interview.	Interviewer sets ground rules, including asking permission to tape-record or videotape or to quote the subject, at the beginning of the interview.	Interviewer sets some ground rules at the beginning of the interview but tries to set others after the interview has started.	Interviewer asks permission to quote the subject at the end of the interview or forgets to set other ground rules.	Interviewer does not set any ground rules and does not ask permission to quote the subject.
Interviewer allows the subject to answer questions completely, without interruptions.	Interviewer listens patiently, allowing the subject to answer all questions completely, without interruptions	Interviewer usually listens patiently, allowing the subject to answer most questions without interruption.	Interviewer interrupts the subject several times, cutting short the subject's answers.	Interviewer dominates the conversation, disagreeing with the subject and giving the interviewer's opinions instead of listening to the subject's answers.
Interviewer asks for explanations and modifies the plan of the interview as appropriate.	Interviewer asks for explanations to clarify points raised during the interview and modifies the plan of the interview as appropriate to get complete information.	Interviewer asks for explanations to clarify several points raised during the interview and sometimes modifies the plan of the interview as appropriate.	Interviewer asks for an explanation to clarify one point raised during the interview or follows up with a related question.	Interviewer does not ask for an explanation of any point raised during the interview and only asks questions on the interviewer's list.
Interviewer keeps the focus on the subject.	Interviewer keeps the focus on the subject throughout the interview.	Interviewer usually keeps the focus on the subject, with few digressions.	Interviewer only occasionally focuses on the subject.	Interviewer goes off on tangents related to the interviewer's experiences but not directly related to the subject.

CRITERIA FOR EVALUATION	SCORE POINT 4	SCORE POINT 3	SCORE POINT 2	SCORE POINT 1
Interviewer courteously wraps up the interview.	Interviewer courteously wraps up the interview at an appropriate point and thanks the subject.	Interviewer courteously wraps up the interview but may let the interview drag on too long.	Interviewer is courteous but lets the interview trail off without a clear ending.	Interviewer ends the interview abruptly or lets the interview drag on so long that the subject ends the interview, and interviewer does not thank the subject.
If necessary, interviewer follows up to check facts after the interview.	Interviewer follows up on all facts that need to be verified following the interview.	Interviewer follows up on several facts that need to be verified following the interview.	Interviewer follows up on at least one fact that needs to be verified following the interview.	Interviewer does not follow up on any fact that needs to be verified following the interview.
Oral Language Conventions				
Standard English is used appropriately for this grade level.	Standard English is used appropriately for this grade level throughout the interview.	Standard English appropriate for this grade level is used, with few problems.	Inconsistent use of standard English jars the subject and the listener.	Minimal use of standard English confuses the subject and the listener.

Scales and Sample Papers

Analytical Scale: 6 Traits—Plus 1

IDEAS AND CONTENT

Score 5

The paper is clear, focused, and engaging. Its thoughtful, concrete details capture the reader's attention and flesh out the central theme, main idea, or story line.

- **A score "5" paper has the following characteristics.**

  ✓ The topic is clearly focused and manageable for a paper of its kind; it is not overly broad or scattered.
  ✓ Ideas are original and creative.
  ✓ The writer appears to be working from personal knowledge or experience.
  ✓ Key details are insightful and well considered; they are not obvious, predictable, or humdrum.
  ✓ The development of the topic is thorough and purposeful; the writer anticipates and answers the reader's questions.
  ✓ Supporting details are never superfluous or merely ornamental; every detail contributes to the whole.

Score 3

The writer develops the topic in a general or basic way; although clear, the paper remains routine or broad.

- **A score "3" paper has the following characteristics.**

  ✓ Although the topic may be fuzzy, it is still possible to understand the writer's purpose and to predict how the paper will be developed.
  ✓ Support is present, but somewhat vague and unhelpful in illustrating the key issues or main idea; the writer makes references to his or her own experience or knowledge but has difficulty moving from general observations to specifics.
  ✓ Ideas are understandable, yet not detailed, elaborated upon, or personalized; the writer's ideas do not reveal any deep comprehension of the topic or of the task.
  ✓ The writer does not stray from the topic, but ideas remain general or slightly implicit; more information is necessary to fill in the gaps.

Score 1

The paper does not exhibit any clear purpose or main idea. The reader must use the scattered details to infer a coherent and meaningful message.

- **A score "1" paper has the following characteristics.**

  ✓ The writer seems not to have truly settled on a topic; the essay reads like a series of brainstorming notes or disconnected, random thoughts.
  ✓ The thesis is a vague statement of the topic rather than a main idea about the topic; in addition, there is little or no support or detail.
  ✓ Information is very limited or vague; readers must make inferences to fill in gaps of logic or to identify any progression of ideas.
  ✓ Text may be rambling and repetitious; alternatively, the length may not be adequate for a thoughtful development of ideas.
  ✓ There is no subordination of ideas; every idea seems equally weighted, or ideas are not tied to a main idea.

Analytical Scale: 6 Traits—Plus 1 *(continued)*

ORGANIZATION

Score 5

Organization enables the clear communication of the central idea or story line. The order of information draws the reader effortlessly through the text.

- **A score "5" paper has the following characteristics.**

  ✓ The sequencing is logical and effective.

  ✓ The essay contains an interesting or inviting introduction and a satisfying conclusion.

  ✓ The pacing is carefully controlled; the writer slows down to provide explanation or elaboration when appropriate and increases the pace when necessary.

  ✓ Transitions carefully connect ideas and cue the reader to specific relationships between ideas.

  ✓ The choice of organizational structure is appropriate to the writer's purpose and audience.

  ✓ If present, the title sums up the central idea of the paper in a fresh or thoughtful way.

Score 3

Organization is reasonably strong; it enables the reader to move continually forward without undue confusion.

- **A score "3" paper has the following characteristics.**

  ✓ The essay has an introduction and conclusion. However, the introduction may not be inviting or engaging; the conclusion may not knit all the paper's ideas together.

  ✓ Sequencing is logical but predictable. Sometimes, the sequence may be so formulaic that it distracts from the content.

  ✓ At times, the sequence may not consistently support the essay's ideas; the reader may wish to reorder sections mentally or to supply transitions as he or she reads.

  ✓ Pacing is reasonably well done, although sometimes the writer moves ahead too quickly or spends too much time on unimportant details.

  ✓ At times, transitions may be fuzzy, showing unclear connections between ideas.

  ✓ If present, the title may be dull or a simple restatement of the topic or prompt.

Score 1

Writing does not exhibit a sense of purpose or writing strategy. Ideas, details, or events appear to be cobbled together without any internal structure.

- **A score "1" paper has the following characteristics.**

  ✓ Sequencing needs work; one idea or event does not logically follow another. Organizational problems make it difficult for the reader to understand the main idea.

  ✓ There is no real introduction to guide the reader into the paper; neither is there any real conclusion or attempt to tie things up at the end.

  ✓ Pacing is halting or inconsistent; the writer may slow the pace or speed up at inappropriate times.

  ✓ Ideas are connected with confusing transitions; alternatively, connections are altogether absent.

  ✓ If present, the title does not accurately reflect the content of the essay.

Analytical Scale: 6 Traits—Plus 1 (continued)

VOICE

Score 5

The writing is expressive and engaging. In addition, the writer seems to have a clear awareness of audience and purpose.

- A score "5" paper has the following characteristics.

  ✓ The tone of the writing is appropriate for the purpose and audience of the paper.
  ✓ The reader is aware of a real person behind the text; if appropriate, the writer takes risks in revealing a personal dimension throughout the piece.
  ✓ If the paper is expository or persuasive, the writer shows a strong connection to the topic and explains why the reader should care about the issue.
  ✓ If the paper is a narrative, the point of view is sincere, interesting, and compelling.

Score 3

The writer is reasonably genuine but does not reveal any excitement or connection with the issue. The resulting paper is pleasant but not truly engaging.

- A score "3" paper has the following characteristics.

  ✓ The writer offers obvious generalities instead of personal insights.
  ✓ The writer uses neutral language and a slightly flattened tone.
  ✓ The writer communicates in an earnest and pleasing manner, yet takes no risks. In only a few instances is the reader captivated or moved.
  ✓ Expository or persuasive writing does not reveal a consistent engagement with the topic; there is no attempt to build credibility with the audience.
  ✓ Narrative writing doesn't reveal a fresh or individual perspective.

Score 1

Writing is mechanical or wooden. The writer appears indifferent to the topic and/or the audience.

- A score "1" paper has the following characteristics.

  ✓ The writer shows no concern with the audience; the voice may be jarringly inappropriate for the intended reader.
  ✓ The development of the topic is so limited that no identifiable point of view is present; or the writing is so short that it offers little but a general introduction of the topic.
  ✓ The writer seems to speak in a monotone, using a voice that suppresses all excitement about the message.
  ✓ Although the writing may communicate on a functional level, the writing is ordinary and takes no risks; depending on the topic, it may be overly technical or jargonistic.

Analytical Scale: 6 Traits—Plus 1 (continued)

WORD CHOICE

Score 5

Words are precise, engaging, and unaffected. They convey the writer's message in an interesting and effective way.

- **A score "5" paper has the following characteristics.**

  ✓ All words are specific and appropriate. In all instances, the writer has taken care to choose the right words or phrases.
  ✓ The paper's language is natural, not overwrought; it never shows a lack of control. Clichés and jargon are rarely used.
  ✓ The paper contains energetic verbs; precise nouns and modifiers provide clarity.
  ✓ The writer uses vivid words and phrases, including sensory details; such language creates distinct images in the reader's mind.

Score 3

Despite its lack of flair, the paper's language gets the message across. It is functional and clear.

- **A score "3" paper has the following characteristics.**

  ✓ Words are correct and generally adequate, but lack originality or precision.
  ✓ Familiar words and phrases do not pique the reader's interest or imagination. Lively verbs and phrases perk things up occasionally, but the paper does not consistently sparkle.
  ✓ There are attempts at engaging or academic language, but they sometimes seem overly showy or pretentious.
  ✓ The writing contains passive verbs and basic nouns and adjectives, and it lacks precise adverbs.

Score 1

The writer's limited vocabulary impedes communication; he or she seems to struggle for words to convey a clear message.

- **A score "1" paper has the following characteristics.**

  ✓ Vague language communicates an imprecise or incomplete message. The reader is left confused or unsure of the writer's purpose.
  ✓ Words are used incorrectly. In addition, frequent misuse of parts of speech impairs understanding.
  ✓ Redundancy in the paper is distracting.
  ✓ The writing overuses jargon or clichés.

Analytical Scale: 6 Traits—Plus 1 *(continued)*

SENTENCE FLUENCY

Score 5

Sentences are thoughtfully constructed, and sentence structure is varied throughout the paper. When read aloud, the writing is fluent and rhythmic.

- ■ A score "5" paper has the following characteristics.

  ✓ The sentences are constructed so that meaning is clear to the reader.

  ✓ Sentences vary in length and in structure.

  ✓ Varied sentence beginnings add interest and clarity.

  ✓ The writing has a steady beat; the reader is able to read the text effortlessly, without confusion or stumbling.

  ✓ Dialogue, if used, is natural. Any fragments are used purposefully and contribute to the paper's style.

  ✓ Thoughtful connectives and transitions between sentences reveal how the paper's ideas work together.

Score 3

The text maintains a steady rhythm, but the reader may find it more flat or mechanical than fluent or musical.

- ■ A score "3" paper has the following characteristics.

  ✓ Sentences are usually grammatical and unified, but they are routine rather than artful. The writer has not paid a great deal of attention to how the sentences sound.

  ✓ There is some variation in sentence length and structure as well as in sentence beginnings. Not all sentences are constructed exactly the same way.

  ✓ The reader may have to search for transitional words and phrases that show how sentences relate to one another. Sometimes, such context clues are entirely absent when they should be present.

  ✓ Although sections of the paper invite expressive oral reading, the reader may also encounter many stilted or awkward sections.

Score 1

The reader will encounter challenges in reading the choppy or confusing text; meaning may be significantly obscured by the errors in sentence construction.

- ■ A score "1" paper has the following characteristics.

  ✓ The sentences do not "hang together." They are run-on, incomplete, monotonous, or awkward.

  ✓ Phrasing often sounds sing-song, not natural. The paper does not invite expressive oral reading.

  ✓ Nearly all the sentences begin the same way, and they may all follow the same pattern (e.g., subject-verb-object). The result may be a monotonous repetition of sounds.

  ✓ Endless connectives or a complete lack of connectives creates a confused muddle of language.

Analytical Scale: 6 Traits—Plus 1 *(continued)*

CONVENTIONS

Score 5

Standard writing conventions (e.g., spelling, punctuation, capitalization, grammar, usage, and paragraphing) are used correctly and in a way that aids the reader's understanding. Any errors tend to be minor; the piece is nearly ready for publication.

- **A score "5" paper has the following characteristics.**
  - ✓ Paragraphing is regular and enhances the organization of the paper.
  - ✓ Grammar and usage are correct and add clarity to the text as a whole. Sometimes, the writer may manipulate conventions in a controlled way—especially grammar and spelling—for stylistic effect.
  - ✓ Punctuation is accurate; it enables the reader to move through the text with understanding and ease.
  - ✓ The writer's understanding of capitalization rules is evident throughout the paper.
  - ✓ Most words, even difficult ones, are spelled correctly.
  - ✓ The writing is long and complex enough to show the writer using a wide range of conventions skillfully.

Score 3

The writer exhibits an awareness of a limited set of standard writing conventions and uses them to enhance the paper's readability. Although the writer shows control, at times errors distract the reader or impede communication. Moderate editing is required for publication.

- **A score "3" paper has the following characteristics.**
  - ✓ Paragraphs are used, but may begin in the wrong places or run together sections that should be separate paragraphs.
  - ✓ Conventions may not always be correct. However, problems with grammar and usage are usually not serious enough to distort meaning.
  - ✓ Terminal (end-of-sentence) punctuation is usually correct; internal punctuation (e.g., commas, apostrophes, semi-colons, parentheses) may be missing or wrong.
  - ✓ Common words are usually spelled correctly.
  - ✓ Most words are capitalized correctly, but the writer's command of more sophisticated capitalization skills is inconsistent.

Score 1

There are errors in spelling, punctuation, usage and grammar, capitalization, and/or paragraphing that seriously impede the reader's comprehension. Extensive editing is required for publication.

- **A score "1" paper has the following characteristics.**
  - ✓ Paragraphing is missing, uneven, or too frequent. Most of the paragraphs do not reinforce or support the organizational structure of the paper.
  - ✓ Errors in grammar/usage are very common and distracting; such errors also affect the paper's meaning.
  - ✓ Punctuation, including terminal punctuation, is often missing or incorrect.
  - ✓ Even common words are frequently misspelled.
  - ✓ Capitalization is haphazard or reveals the writer's understanding of only the simplest rules.
  - ✓ The paper must be read once just to decode the language and then again to capture the paper's meaning.

Analytical Scale: 6 Traits—Plus 1 *(continued)*

PRESENTATION

Score 5

The presentation of the writing is clear and visually appealing. The format helps the reader focus on the message of the writing.

■ A score "5" paper has the following characteristics.

✓ If the paper is handwritten, all letters are formed clearly, and the slant and spacing are consistent.

✓ If the paper is word processed, fonts and font sizes are appropriate for the genre of writing and assist the reader's comprehension.

✓ White space and text are balanced.

✓ Text markers, such as title, headings, and numbering, highlight important information and aid reading of the text.

✓ If visuals are used, they are appropriate to the writing, are integrated effectively with the text, and clearly communicate and enhance the message.

Score 3

The presentation of the writing is readable and understandable; however, inconsistencies in format at times detract from the text.

■ A score "3" paper has the following characteristics.

✓ If the paper is handwritten, the handwriting is legible, but some inconsistencies occur in spacing and the formation and slant of letters.

✓ If the paper is word processed, fonts and font sizes are inconsistent, sometimes distracting the reader.

✓ White space and text are consistent, although a different use of space would make the paper easier to read.

✓ Text markers, such as title, headings, and numbering, are used to some degree; however, they are inconsistent and only occasionally helpful to the reader.

✓ Visuals are sometimes ineffective and not clearly linked to the text.

Score 1

The presentation and format of the writing are confusing, making the paper difficult to read and understand.

■ A score "1" paper has the following characteristics.

✓ If the paper is handwritten, the letters are formed incorrectly or irregularly. The uneven slant and spacing make the paper difficult to read.

✓ If the paper is word processed, fonts and font sizes are used randomly or inappropriately, disrupting the reader's comprehension.

✓ Spacing appears random, with use of white space either excessive or minimal.

✓ Text markers, such as title, headings, and numbering, are not used.

✓ Visuals are inaccurate, inappropriate, misleading, or confusing.

Holistic Scale: Four Points
Fictional or Autobiographical Writing

Score 4

This high-quality writing develops plot, characters, and setting with sensory details and concrete language. The writing is noticeably clear and coherent.

- *The writing strongly demonstrates*
  - ✓ thorough attention to all parts of the writing task
  - ✓ a clear understanding of purpose and audience
  - ✓ a consistent point of view, focus, and organizational structure, including effective use of transitions
  - ✓ a clear central idea with relevant facts, details, and/or explanations
  - ✓ a well-developed plot line, complex major and minor characters, and a definite setting
  - ✓ use of appropriate strategies such as dialogue, suspense, and narrative action
  - ✓ a variety of sentence types
  - ✓ proficiency in the conventions of the English language (grammar, punctuation, capitalization, spelling). The few errors do not interfere with the reader's understanding of the writing.

Score 3

The writing develops plot, characters, and setting with relevant details. For the most part, writing is clear and coherent.

- *The writing generally demonstrates*
  - ✓ attention to all parts of the writing task
  - ✓ understanding of purpose and audience
  - ✓ a consistent point of view, focus, and organizational structure, including the effective use of some transitions
  - ✓ a central idea with mostly relevant facts, details, and/or explanations
  - ✓ an adequately developed plot line, major and minor characters, and a definite setting
  - ✓ use of appropriate strategies such as dialogue, suspense, and narrative action
  - ✓ a variety of sentence types
  - ✓ proficiency in the conventions of the English language (grammar, punctuation, capitalization, spelling). The few errors do not interfere with the reader's understanding of the writing.

Score 2

The writing only marginally develops plot, characters, and setting.

- *The writing demonstrates*
  - ✓ attention to only parts of the writing task
  - ✓ little understanding of purpose and audience
  - ✓ an inconsistent point of view, focus, and/or organizational structure, including ineffective or awkward transitions
  - ✓ a poorly developed central idea with limited facts, details, and/or explanations
  - ✓ minimal development of plot line, characters, and setting
  - ✓ use of some strategies such as dialogue, suspense, and narrative action, but with minimal effectiveness

✓ little variety in sentence types

✓ inconsistent use of the conventions of the English language (grammar, punctuation, capitalization, spelling). Several errors may interfere with the reader's understanding of the writing.

Score 1

The writing is an unsuccessful attempt at creating a narrative.

▪ *The writing lacks*

✓ attention to most parts of the writing task

✓ understanding of purpose and audience

✓ a point of view, focus, organizational structure, and transitions

✓ a central idea but may contain marginally related facts, details, and/or explanations

✓ a developed plot line

✓ use of strategies such as dialogue, suspense, and narrative action

✓ sentence variety

✓ basic proficiency in the conventions of the English language (grammar, punctuation, capitalization, spelling). The numerous errors interfere with the reader's understanding of the writing.

Sample A
Fictional Writing: Short Story

> **PROMPT**
>
> A successful short story has a well-developed plot, believable characters, and a specific setting. Think about a character who has a problem that must be solved. Write a short story that is full of suspense and will be interesting to readers your own age.

As Neal angrily jammed the hairpin into the fragile lock of his sister's journal, he concentrated on what she had done to him. He had considered ripping the lock right off the book, but he knew better. As the lock popped open, undamaged, Neal congratulated himself on his perfect plan. He would find some juicy secrets and pass them around school. All he could think about was how his sister had borrowed his new bike and wrecked it, badly scratching the flawless blue metallic paint.

Just as Neal opened the book, the sound of footsteps in the hallway made him jump, and he almost dropped the book. The footsteps stopped at the hall closet and then returned to the living room. "This was a mistake," thought Neal. "What'll I do if someone catches me?" Still, he had come this far; he might as well finish what he had planned. He looked down at the open book in his hands. His sister's diary was neatly written, with small drawings on each page. As he turned the pages, Neal found himself in a secret world where he knew he didn't belong. "I shouldn't be reading this," he said to himself. Along with all the other predictable secrets, he learned that it was his sister, not his parents, who had taken his drawing out of the trash and entered it in the local art contest. That's how he won second place and the prize, his new bike.

Just when Neal was about to close the journal, the latest entry leaped out at him. He read, "Everything went wrong today. At Dooley's, I dropped some really expensive nail polish I was looking at and the bottle shattered. What a mess! I sneaked out and

Sample A *(continued)*

then, believe it or not, ran Neal's bike into a tree on my way home. Somehow I have to pay for both, but Neal loves that bike. What if it's never the same?'"

Neal suddenly remembered why he was in her room, but it no longer mattered.

Three days later Neal's sister opened a letter with no return address. She read, "I saw you break something in Dooley's last weekend. I bought a bottle of the same polish and then put it back on the shelf. Here's the receipt. I am doing this because someone once did something nice for me. A friend"

Sample A Evaluation
Fictional Writing: Short Story

Four-Point Holistic Scale

Rating: 4 points

Comments: The story thoroughly addresses all parts of the writing task and demonstrates a clear understanding of purpose and audience. The well-developed plot reveals the personalities of Neal and his sister, the conflict that initiates the action, and the resolution, which reveals a universal lesson. Dialogue, suspense, and narrative action are used skillfully and realistically to develop the story. Point of view is consistent, and the story maintains its focus, using effective transitions to produce a coherent organizational structure. Details and explanations are skillfully and vividly presented, using specific words that give the reader a clear picture of the action and scene. The writer uses a variety of sentence types and demonstrates proficiency in the conventions of the English language.

6 Traits—Plus 1 Analytical Scale

Ratings (High score is 5.)

Ideas and Content: 5	**Sentence Fluency: 5**
Organization: 5	**Conventions: 5**
Voice: 5	**Presentation: 4**
Word Choice: 5	

Comments:

Ideas and Content: An overarching idea governs the story. The reader receives a clear idea of Neal's character and also of his sister's.

Organization: The organizational structure effectively incorporates internal dialogue and suspense to move the plot along, and the story builds to an effective and original resolution.

Voice: The writer's voice is clear and engaging and demonstrates a thoughtful approach to the writing task.

Word Choice: Word choice is specific, effective, and sometimes inspired.

Sentence Fluency: The story uses a variety of sentence types, creating a fluid reading experience, alternately speeding up or slowing down the action as appropriate.

Conventions: The writer demonstrates a strong command of the conventions of the English language.

Presentation: The presentation is clear, simple, and easy to read.

Sample B
Fictional Writing: Short Story

PROMPT

A successful short story has a well-developed plot, believable characters, and a specific setting. Think about a character who has a problem that must be solved. Write a short story that is full of suspense and will be interesting to readers your own age.

As Neal pushed the hairpin into the lock of his sister's journal, he thought of what she did to him. He had wanted to rip the lock right off the book, but he knew better. When the lock popped open, unbroke, Neal was glad. He would find some of his sister's secrets and tell everybody at school. He was mad at her, because she had borrowed his new bike and wrecked it, scratching the paint.

As he turned the pages of the book, Neal knew he shouldn't be there. "I shouldn't be reading this," he said to himself. Along with all the other secrets, he learned that it was his sister, not his parents, who had taken his drawing out of the trash and entered it in the local contest. That's how he won the new bike.

Then he saw the latest entry. He read, "Everything went wrong today. At Dooley's, I dropped some really expensive nail polish I was looking at and the bottle shattered. What a mess! I sneaked out and then believe it or not ran Neal's bike into a tree on my way home. Somehow I have to pay for both, but Neal loves that bike. What if it's never the same?"

Then Neal remembered why he was in her room but he changed his mind and decided to do something different. His sister wasn't so bad after all.

Three days later Neal's sister opened a letter with no return address. The letter said, "I saw you break something in the store last week. Here is the receipt for it. I bought a bottle of the same polish. I am doing this because someone once did something nice for me. A friend"

Sample B Evaluation
Fictional Writing: Short Story

Four-Point Holistic Scale

Rating: 3 points

Comments: The story addresses all parts of the writing task and demonstrates an understanding of purpose and audience. The plot reveals the personalities of Neal and his sister, the conflict that initiates the action, and the resolution. Some elements of the plot, such as the resolution revealed in the letter, need more specificity and a better connection to the central idea. Dialogue, suspense, and narrative action are used appropriately to develop the story. Point of view is consistent, and the story maintains its focus, often using effective transitions to produce a relatively coherent organizational structure. Suspenseful elements are undermined by the fourth paragraph, which telegraphs the resolution. Most details and explanations are skillfully and vividly presented, using specific words that give the reader a clear picture of the action and scene. The writer uses a variety of sentence types and demonstrates proficiency in the conventions of the English language.

6 Traits—Plus 1 Analytical Scale

Ratings (High score is 5.)

Ideas and Content: 4	**Sentence Fluency: 4**
Organization: 3	**Conventions: 3**
Voice: 4	**Presentation: 4**
Word Choice: 3	

Comments:

Ideas and Content: The writer develops a clear idea for the story's theme.

Organization: Organizational structure of the plot is generally consistent, but the fourth paragraph undermines the suspense of the resolution by including statements about Neal's future actions and his changed attitude toward his sister. All plot elements contribute to the central idea, but connections between some elements and the central idea need more specificity.

Voice: The writer's voice is consistent but not particularly engaging.

Word Choice: Word choice is appropriate but often general; more specific, vivid words are needed for a higher score.

Sentence Fluency: Varied sentence types are used appropriately, creating a relatively interesting reading rhythm.

Conventions: The writer demonstrates general proficiency in the conventions of the English language. The few errors do not interfere with the reader's understanding of the writing.

Presentation: The story is presented in consistent and readable form.

Sample C
Fictional Writing: Short Story

PROMPT

A successful short story has a well-developed plot, believable characters, and a specific setting. Think about a character who has a problem that must be solved. Write a short story that is full of suspense and will be interesting to readers your own age.

Neal broke into his sister's diary. He was carfull not to brake the lock. He picked it because he didn't want her to find out. He was mad because she busted his new bike. She took it without asking and racked it and messed up the paint. So he was going to find out her secrits and tell everbody. That'd show her.

He was afraid someone will see him. I wish I wasn't here. What if my sister comes back and sees me? Anyway, the book was boring. She just writes boring stuff. But he found out his sister took his picture out of the trash. He was thinking his parents took his picture to the art contest. His sister did it. Thats how he got the bike. So she wasn't so bad. So he want tell her secrits. He's still mad she racked his bike. He hopes she want find out he read her book. Sisters can be O.K., but he still wants his bike fixed.

Sample C Evaluation
Fictional Writing: Short Story

Four-Point Holistic Scale

Rating: 2 points

Comments: The story addresses only parts of the writing task. The plot, characters, and setting are only minimally developed. The writing demonstrates little understanding of purpose and audience. Point of view is inconsistent, alternating between third and first person. Ineffective or missing transitions detract from the coherence of the story and force the reader to fill in gaps in the plot. Limited details and explanations result in a poorly developed central idea. An attempt at using suspense is minimally effective, and dialogue cannot be identified. It is unclear whether several sentences in the second paragraph are an attempt at dialogue, incorrectly punctuated, or a shift in point of view. There is some variety in sentence types, but most sentences are short and choppy. The conventions of the English language are used inconsistently and sometimes interfere with the reader's understanding.

6 Traits—Plus 1 Analytical Scale

Ratings (High score is 5.)

Ideas and Content: 2	**Sentence Fluency: 2**
Organization: 2	**Conventions: 2**
Voice: 1	**Presentation: 4**
Word Choice: 2	

Comments:

Ideas and Content: The story includes a poorly developed central idea; nevertheless, the reader has no trouble identifying the idea. Limited details present only a sketchy plot, characters, and setting.

Organization: Organizational structure is hampered by ineffective or missing transitions that force the reader to fill in gaps. The story demonstrates minimal understanding of appropriate organizational strategies.

Voice: Shifting point of view results in a confusing, inconsistent voice that demonstrates little understanding of purpose and audience.

Word Choice: Word choice is simplistic and vague, preventing the reader from picturing the action or scene.

Sentence Fluency: Most sentences are short and choppy, but there are a few varied sentence types.

Conventions: Inconsistent use of the conventions of the English language sometimes interferes with the reader's understanding of the writing.

Presentation: Although the writer has not created an engaging story, the presentation is neat and clear to the reader.

Holistic Scale: Four Points
Response to Literature

Score 4

This insightful interpretation of literature develops a clear central idea with important textual evidence. The writing indicates a careful reading and coherent organization.

- **The writing strongly demonstrates**

  ✓ thorough attention to all parts of the writing task
  ✓ a clear understanding of purpose and audience
  ✓ a thoughtful, comprehensive grasp of the text
  ✓ a consistent point of view, focus, and organizational structure, including effective use of transitions
  ✓ organization of accurate and coherent interpretations based on the literary work
  ✓ a clear central idea with relevant facts and/or explanations
  ✓ use of specific textual examples and details to support the interpretation
  ✓ a variety of sentence types
  ✓ proficiency in the conventions of the English language (grammar, punctuation, capitalization, spelling). The few errors do not interfere with the reader's understanding of the writing.

Score 3

The interpretation of literature develops a central idea with textual evidence. The writing indicates understanding of the literary work.

- **The writing generally demonstrates**

  ✓ attention to all parts of the writing task
  ✓ understanding of purpose and audience
  ✓ a comprehensive grasp of the text
  ✓ a consistent point of view, focus, and organizational structure, including the effective use of some transitions
  ✓ organization of accurate and reasonably coherent interpretations around clear ideas from the literary work
  ✓ a central idea with mostly relevant facts, details, and/or explanations
  ✓ use of some textual examples and details to support the interpretations
  ✓ a variety of sentence types
  ✓ proficiency in the conventions of the English language (grammar, punctuation, capitalization, spelling). The few errors do not interfere with the reader's understanding of the writing.

Score 2

The interpretation of literature is largely unsupported with textual evidence. Inaccuracies indicate limited understanding.

- **The writing demonstrates**

  ✓ attention to only parts of the writing task
  ✓ little understanding of purpose and audience
  ✓ a limited grasp of the text
  ✓ an inconsistent point of view, focus, and/or organizational structure, including ineffective or awkward transitions
  ✓ a poorly developed central idea with limited facts, details, and/or explanations

Holistic Scale *(continued)*

✓ interpretations that lack accuracy or coherence as related to ideas from the literary work

✓ use of few, if any, textual examples and details to support the interpretations

✓ little variety in sentence types

✓ inconsistent use of the conventions of the English language (grammar, punctuation, capitalization, spelling). The occasional errors may interfere with the reader's understanding of the writing.

Score 1

The writing is mainly a retelling of the literary work. The writer shows minimal understanding.

■ *The writing lacks*

✓ attention to most parts of the writing task

✓ understanding of purpose and audience

✓ a firm grasp of the text

✓ a point of view, focus, organizational structure, and transitions

✓ a central idea but may contain marginally related facts, details, and/or explanations

✓ an interpretation or may simply summarize the literature

✓ textual examples and details

✓ sentence variety

✓ basic proficiency in the conventions of the English language (grammar, punctuation, capitalization, spelling). The numerous errors interfere with the reader's understanding of the writing.

Sample A: Response to Literature

PROMPT

Think about a fictional character who has interested you. Write a well-organized paper analyzing that character for your classmates to read. Remember to include any important problems the character solves or overcomes. What does the character learn? Give details from the story to support your ideas.

Do you ever have trouble feeling that you "fit in"? Have you ever felt that no matter how hard you tried, you couldn't satisfy other people? Craig, a Chinese American teenager, faces these problems in Laurence Yep's <u>Sea Glass</u>. Although Craig knows that he is intelligent, events happen in the story that make Craig feel lonely and rejected, as if he is an outsider at school. He is persistent in his efforts to please people, especially his own father.

School is a nightmare because Craig feels that he does not fit in with the other students. He and his family recently have moved from San Francisco's Chinatown where he felt that he belonged. Here in Concepcion, however, his efforts to fit in bring him nothing but painful rejection. Even his own cousin Sheila makes fun of him. As his cousin, Sheila should be supportive and helpful. Instead, she and her mean friends insult him for being fat, having short hair, and wearing odd clothes. Craig can't seem to stand up for himself. He is hurt by the other students' behavior.

Craig thinks that he can't measure up at home. Although he is persistent and continues to make an effort, he can't seem to please anyone, especially his father. Craig doesn't think he has the necessary ability to excel in sports, but his dad doesn't seem to care that Craig feels this way. His dad wants him to do well in sports, as he did when he was a student. Craig practices sports and tries to become a better athlete, but he does not enjoy it.

Even though Craig feels insecure among his classmates and feels that his father doesn't accept him as he is, Craig has his own strengths. For one thing, he is intelligent. He enjoys school subjects other than P.E. He says that in the classroom he can be sure

Sample A *(continued)*

of himself and have things become clear for a while. He is smart enough to do well in school and to prepare himself for a better life.

Just because you can't seem to satisfy others now doesn't mean that later in life you won't succeed. Craig is intelligent and does well in his school subjects. This helps him make up for the way he is treated by his classmates, and someday Craig's father will accept Craig for himself. Craig's persistence will help him develop his own way to shine in the world. Someday, Craig will experience life in a happier way.

Sample A Evaluation: Response to Literature

Four-Point Holistic Scale

Rating: 4 points

Comments: The paper clearly addresses all parts of the writing task and develops thoughtful interpretations that demonstrate a comprehensive grasp of the text. The organizational structure is clear and complete, with the central idea stated in the introduction, supported in the body paragraphs, and restated in the conclusion. The conclusion also extends the thesis, drawing a universal lesson from the character development revealed in the literary work. The organizational structure, point of view, and focus are consistent, and transitions effectively link all ideas. Accurate details from the literary selection are skillfully used to support the analysis. The writer uses a variety of sentence types and chooses effective, precise words. Rhetorical questions in the introduction skillfully grab the reader's attention. The writer's voice is clear and engaging throughout. The paper demonstrates a thorough command of written conventions appropriate for this grade level.

6 Traits—Plus 1 Analytical Scale

Ratings (High score is 5.)

Ideas and Content: 5	**Sentence Fluency: 5**
Organization: 5	**Conventions: 5**
Voice: 5	**Presentation: 4**
Word Choice: 5	

Comments:

Ideas and Content: The paper is clearly focused on the character analysis. The writer provides specific textual details to support each element of the analysis.

Organization: Organizational structure is logical and coherent, and the topic sentences in the introduction and the body paragraphs prepare the reader for what is to come.

Voice: The writer's voice is engaging and appropriate for the interpretative purpose, and the writer demonstrates a clear understanding of purpose and audience.

Word Choice: Word choice is very good. The writer uses energetic verbs and precise words and phrases to describe Craig's emotions and the conflict he faces.

Sentence Fluency: Sentence structure is varied, creating an easy-to-read rhythm and helping emphasize important points. Rhetorical questions are skillfully used to grab the reader's attention.

Conventions: The writer demonstrates a very good understanding of the conventions of written language.

Presentation: The presentation is simple and direct with no distracting flourishes.

Sample B: Response to Literature

PROMPT

Think about a fictional character who has interested you. Write a well-organized paper analyzing that character for your classmates to read. Remember to include any important problems the character solves or overcomes. What does the character learn? Give details from the story to support your ideas.

Have you ever felt that no matter how hard you try, you couldn't satisfy other people? These are the problems Craig, a Chinese American teenager, faces in Laurence Yep's Sea Glass. Things happen that make Craig feel he doesn't belong and can't please anyone, even though he is a good person. The people at school and home aren't helping a bit.

School is a nightmare. He and his family used to live in San Francisco's Chinatown. He felt that he belonged there. In Concepcion, where they live now, he feels he doesn't belong. Even his own cousin Sheila makes fun of him. She and her mean friends insult him for being fat, short hair, and odd clothes. They call him names. Craig can't seem to stand up for himself.

Home is no better. Craig can't seem to please anyone, especially his father. Craig doesn't think he is good in sports, but his dad doesn't seem to care. His dad wants him to be good at sports, like him.

He doesn't understand why anyone is mean. He tried to be honest and answer other students' questions, but they keep picking on him. He felt upset and unhappy but he is strong, too. Because, he is intelligent. He says in the classroom he can be sure of himself and have things become clear for a while.

Craig feels like an outsider. But he is intelligent and kind. He knows that he is a good and valueable person. He will develop his own way and will be happier someday.

Sample B Evaluation: Response to Literature

Four-Point Holistic Scale

Rating: 3 points

Comments: The paper addresses all parts of the writing task. The organizational structure is consistent and sometimes uses effective transitions. Accurate and appropriate textual references support the writer's analysis and interpretation. The analysis of character is rather general and suffers from a lack of specific detail. Many sentences are short and choppy. The writer's voice is clear and consistent but not particularly engaging. Word choice is sometimes effective but often trite and repetitive. The writer has general control of the conventions of written language, as characterized by few punctuation and grammar errors.

6 Traits—Plus 1 Analytical Scale

Ratings (High score is 5.)

Ideas and Content: 4	**Sentence Fluency: 3**
Organization: 4	**Conventions: 3**
Voice: 3	**Presentation: 4**
Word Choice: 3	

Comments:

Ideas and Content: The paper develops a clear analysis of character, but it lacks specificity and fluency. Accurate textual references effectively support the analysis of each element of the analysis, but most references lack necessary details.

Organization: The organizational structure is clear and consistent, with the first three body paragraphs examining problems at school and at home and the fourth body paragraph indicating how the character tries to solve these problems.

Voice: The writer's voice is clear and consistent but not particularly engaging.

Word Choice: Word choice is occasionally effective but often trite and repetitive, though never inappropriate.

Sentence Fluency: The writer uses a variety of sentence types, but many short, choppy sentences detract from the fluency of the paper.

Conventions: The writer has general control of the conventions of written language; the few spelling, punctuation, and grammar errors do not interfere with the reader's understanding of the paper.

Presentation: The presentation of the paper is consistent and easy to read.

Sample C: Response to Literature

PROMPT

Think about a fictional character who has interested you. Write a well-organized paper analyzing that character for your classmates to read. Remember to include any important problems the character solves or overcomes. What does the character learn? Give details from the story to support your ideas.

In Laurence Yep's <u>Sea Glass</u>, Craig, a Chinese American teenager, feels he don't belong and can't please anyone, even though he is a good person. The people at school and home isn't helping.

Craig is unhappy at school. He feels he don't fit in with the other students. He use to feel he belonged. That was when he livd in San Francisco's Chinatown. He fell he belonged there. Now he livd in Concepcion, he feels he doesn't belong. His own cousin Sheila make fun of him. She and her mean friends tease him. They call him names. Craig don't stand up for hisself.

Home is bad, too. No one seems to like Craig, not even his father. Craig don't think he is good in sports, but his dad don't seem to care.

He doesn't see why anyone has to be mean. Other students pick on him. He won't pick on them, even if he can. They hurt Craig's feelings. But he is smart. He feels good in class. Things make sense to him there.

Craig feels like he don't belong. But he is smart and kind. He knows he is a good person. He will grow up and someday be happy.

Sample C Evaluation: Response to Literature

Four-Point Holistic Scale

Rating: 2 points

Comments: The paper addresses only part of the writing task. The writer states a general interpretation in the introduction and restates it in the conclusion, but most of the development is in the form of a plot summary, with no connection established between plot events and character development. Because of a lack of transitions, connections between details and ideas are not established. There are a few varied sentence types, but most sentences are short and choppy. The paper demonstrates little understanding of purpose and audience. Errors in spelling, punctuation, and grammar interfere with the reader's understanding of the interpretation.

6 Traits—Plus 1 Analytical Scale

Ratings (High score is 5.)

Ideas and Content: 2	**Sentence Fluency: 2**
Organization: 2	**Conventions: 2**
Voice: 2	**Presentation: 4**
Word Choice: 2	

Comments:

Ideas and Content: Information is not always connected to the central idea of the paper. The role of stated plot events in the development of Craig's character is not made clear but must be inferred by the reader. The paper provides only a minimal amount of support.

Organization: Lack of transitions and development makes the organizational structure inconsistent and confusing. There is a clear attempt to write an introduction and a conclusion.

Voice: The paper is too short to allow full development of the writer's voice, though the minimal level of writing indicates a pleasant but unmemorable voice.

Word Choice: Word choice is imprecise, simplistic, and sometimes inappropriate.

Sentence Fluency: Sentence structure is usually short and choppy, with frequent distracting structural errors, but there are several sentence types.

Conventions: Numerous errors in punctuation and grammar interfere with the reader's understanding of the interpretation.

Presentation: The presentation is clear, neat, and focused on the message in spite of the lack of substance of the writing.

Holistic Scale: Four Points
Persuasion

Score 4

This persuasive writing supports a strong position with ample, relevant reasons and evidence. The writer anticipates reader concerns and clearly addresses them.

- *The writing strongly demonstrates*

  ✓ thorough attention to all parts of the writing task
  ✓ a clear understanding of purpose and audience
  ✓ a clear central idea with relevant facts, details, and/or explanations
  ✓ a clearly stated position
  ✓ authoritative defense of a position with specific and relevant evidence and convincing attention to the reader's concerns and point of view
  ✓ a consistent point of view, focus, and organizational structure, including effective use of transitions
  ✓ a variety of sentence types
  ✓ a very good command of the English language (grammar, punctuation, capitalization, spelling). The few errors do not interfere with the reader's understanding of the writing.

Score 3

This persuasive writing supports a position with relevant evidence. The writer addresses reader concerns.

- *The writing generally demonstrates*

  ✓ attention to all parts of the writing task
  ✓ understanding of purpose and audience
  ✓ a consistent point of view, focus, and organizational structure, including the effective use of some transitions
  ✓ a central idea with mostly relevant facts, details, and/or explanations
  ✓ defense of a position with relevant evidence and attention to the reader's concerns and point of view
  ✓ a variety of sentence types
  ✓ proficiency in the conventions of the English language (grammar, punctuation, capitalization, spelling). The few errors do not interfere with the reader's understanding of the writing.

Score 2

This persuasive writing presents a position but includes little relevant evidence.

- *The writing demonstrates*

  ✓ attention to only parts of the writing task
  ✓ little understanding of purpose and audience
  ✓ an inconsistent point of view, focus, and/or organizational structure, including ineffective or awkward transitions
  ✓ a poorly developed central idea with limited facts, details, and/or explanations
  ✓ defense of a position with little, if any, evidence and little attention to reader's concerns and point of view
  ✓ little variety in sentence types
  ✓ inconsistent use of the conventions of the English language (grammar, punctuation, capitalization, spelling). The occasional errors may interfere with the reader's understanding of the writing.

Holistic Scale *(continued)*

Score 1	■ *The writing lacks*
The writing presents a position but does not support it.	✓ attention to most parts of the writing task
	✓ understanding of purpose and audience
	✓ a point of view, focus, organizational structure, and transitions
	✓ a central idea but may contain marginally related facts, details, and/or explanations
	✓ a defense of a position with evidence and fails to address the reader's concerns and point of view
	✓ sentence variety
	✓ basic proficiency in the conventions of the English language (grammar, punctuation, capitalization, spelling). The numerous errors interfere with the reader's understanding of the writing.

STUDENT MODEL

Sample A: Persuasion

PROMPT

Imagine that a local builder found an ancient campsite while clearing land to build a badly needed school. Should the builder be allowed to proceed, or should building stop while archaeologists study the site? Local schools are overcrowded, and archaeologists estimate it could take as long as a year to complete their study. Write an essay for your school paper stating your position and supporting it with convincing reasons.

If construction of a new school for our city is suspended for a year, as archaeologists want, some classes in our old school will have fifty or more students next year. I know it is important to make discoveries at the ancient campsite, but I think a year is too long to wait to start building a new school. I think we should give the archaeologists a shorter time to dig so we don't spend another whole school year crowded into an old school building. My reasons are that technology can help both projects get done faster and that people on both sides want the best for history and for children.

Technology can help in two ways. I think the archaeologists should get one of those scanners that lets them look underground. If they see anything out of the ordinary, they should start digging immediately. If they find nothing in a period of 5 months, we should start to build the foundation for our new school. During the time when the archaeologists are looking at the site, the new school can be designed and we can use computer programs to plan all of the materials that will be needed and figure out the most efficient way to do the job. That way, as soon as the archaeologists finish, we can be ready to start work right away and finish the school faster.

If I was an archaeologist, of course I would want to dig up whatever is down there. They might learn more about early humans or maybe even find something that can confirm the way the dinosaurs died, and then they would want to keep digging. But even if I was an archaeologist, I would probably still want the best for the children. After all, archaeologists probably have kids, too. The archaeologists should try to finish their project as soon as they can so that the school will be ready by the next school

Sample A (continued)

year. If I was an archaeologist I would not want my work to force kids to stay crowded in their old school.

If I was an administrator, obviously I would want to build the school, but I would probably be interested in finding out what was at the site. If there were fossils or artifacts to be found I would have the archaeologists start digging. Their discoveries might give us further things to study in our new school, and our school would be recognized as the place where an important discovery was made. Finding fossils at our new school will give us an advantage, but stopping construction for a whole year would mean the old school will still be crowded and will need extra teachers to provide supervision for the students.

The best solution to this problem is to limit the delay caused by digging at the site. The archaeologists and builders should use technology to speed up the process so construction of the new school can begin in time for the school to be ready for the next school year. We deserve to go to a new school that is not overcrowded.

Sample A Evaluation: Persuasion

Four-Point Holistic Scale

Rating: 4 points

Comments: The writer provides two relevant reasons to defend the stated position. In the first, the writer demonstrates a broad view of the situation, and in the second reason the writer considers multiple perspectives, focusing on the concerns about history and children that both sides share. Ideas are thoughtful, wide-ranging, and organized clearly. The writer demonstrates control of English language conventions. Although the writing might have been a bit more concise, sentences are clear and varied.

6 Traits—Plus 1 Analytical Scale

Ratings (High score is 5.)

Ideas and Content: 4   **Sentence Fluency: 5**

Organization: 4   **Conventions: 5**

Voice: 4   **Presentation: 4**

Word Choice: 3

Comments:

Ideas and Content: The writer identifies a clear position and considers multiple perspectives, although the ideas sometimes lack specificity.

Organization: Organization fits the writer's purpose, and ideas progress logically.

Voice: The writer demonstrates a keen involvement with the topic, but uses a fair and calm voice as he discusses possible concerns from opposing viewpoints.

Word Choice: Word choice is correct and adequate to communicate the writer's ideas.

Sentence Fluency: Sentences vary in length and structure and clearly communicate the writer's message.

Conventions: The writer demonstrates control over the conventions of written language; paragraphing, grammar, punctuation, capitalization, and spelling are generally correct.

Presentation: The format is simple to read and has no distracting features.

Sample B: Persuasion

PROMPT

Imagine that a local builder found an ancient campsite while clearing land to build a badly needed school. Should the builder be allowed to proceed, or should building stop while archaeologists study the site? Local schools are overcrowded, and archaeologists estimate it could take as long as a year to complete their study. Write an essay for your school paper stating your position and supporting it with convincing reasons.

If my school was in this position, I would say that we can't wait a whole year to start building a new school. I would tell the archaeologists to get one of those scanners that lets them look underground. If they find nothing in a period of 5 months, I would tell them you have till the end of the day to get all of your equipment off this proper- ty. Then the administrator's office should bring loads of dirt to fill in what the archae- ologists dug up. After waiting about a week for the dirt to settle in the ground, they could start to build the formation for the school.

If I was a archaeologist, of course I would want to dig whatever is down there. They might find something that can confirm the way the dinousours died, and then they would want to keep digging. But even if I was a archaeologist, I would probably still want the best for the children. The archaeologist should try to finish their project as soon as they can so that the school will be ready by the next school year.

If I was a administrator, I would want to build the school, but I would probably be interested in finding out what was at the site. Any discoveries might give us further things to study in our new school. Finding fossils at our new school will give us an advantage, but stopping construction for a whole year would mean the old school will still be crowded and will need extra teachers to provide supervision for the students. In a way I understand both sides because they both have advantages. The smart decision is to limit the delay caused by digging at the site.

Sample B Evaluation: Persuasion

Four-Point Holistic Scale

Rating: 2 points

Comments: At first, it appears that the writer takes a strong stand, but the defense of that position ends and shifts to the other side. In addition, too much of the paper lists the steps the writer recommends. Organization is logical, and sentences are generally complete. Ideas and word choice are vague and general rather than detailed and specific. Errors in spelling, capitalization, punctuation, and grammar are minor and do not interfere with understanding.

6 Traits—Plus 1 Analytical Scale

Ratings (High score is 5.)

Ideas and Content: 3   **Sentence Fluency: 3**

Organization: 3   **Conventions: 3**

Voice: 3   **Presentation: 4**

Word Choice: 3

Comments:

Ideas and Content: The writer addresses the topic and provides clear, but not detailed, ideas.

Organization: Organization is logical, although the introduction and conclusion are weak and connections between ideas are sometimes unclear.

Voice: The writer's voice, while pleasant, shows a detachment from the topic, and there is no attempt to reveal a consistent or forceful personality to the reader.

Word Choice: Word choice is generally correct and adequate.

Sentence Fluency: Sentences are usually grammatical and vary in structure somewhat.

Conventions: Some paragraphing is missing at the paper's beginning and end, but errors in grammar and spelling do not interfere with the writer's meaning.

Presentation: The clear, simple presentation is accessible to the reader.

Sample C: Persuasion

PROMPT

Imagine that a local builder found an ancient campsite while clearing land to build a badly needed school. Should the builder be allowed to proceed, or should building stop while archaeologists study the site? Local schools are overcrowded, and archaeologists estimate it could take as long as a year to complete their study. Write an essay for your school paper stating your position and supporting it with convincing reasons.

If my school was in this position I would have to say to the archeologist for them to get one of those scanners and look underground. If they find nothing, I would tell them you have till the end of the day to get all of your equipment off this property. Then I would call the administrators office and tell them to bring so many loads of dirt to fill in what the archeologist dug up and then wait about a week for the dirt to settle. The dirt has to settle or the building wont be steady.

If I was a archeologist of course I would want to dig what ever is down there. I would want to hurry an get the project over with so that they could start building the new school for the kids so they wont be crowded in there old school.

If I was a administrator I would want to build the school but if there are fossils maybe we should build the school somewhere else. There is an empty shopping center not to far from our school that we could tear down. Then the archoelogists could dig.

That's what you have to think about will it bring advantages or disadvantages. Now you think which one would you want to be, a archeologist or an administrator. To be an administrator you can't approve that kids can bring knifes and guns to school. To be an archeologist you also have to make smart decisions like if it is the right place to dig to pull arterfacts up or it will be broke, things like that. That is what I think about this. By the way I am for both sides because they both have good advantages.

Sample C Evaluation: Persuasion

Four-Point Holistic Scale

Rating: 1 point

Comments: The writing attempts to be persuasive in nature, but the writer never chooses a position on the topic. The paper drifts into explaining steps and then provides a significant digression about archaeologists and administrators rather than providing support for a persuasive position. The writer does attempt an organizational structure, but ideas are so poorly developed that the paper remains thoroughly confusing. The attempt at addressing another side of the issue is misdirected. The writer demonstrates a limited control over the conventions of English language.

6 Traits—Plus 1 Analytical Scale

Ratings (High score is 5.)

Ideas and Content: 1	**Sentence Fluency: 2**
Organization: 2	**Conventions: 2**
Voice: 1	**Presentation: 4**
Word Choice: 1	

Comments:

Ideas and Content: The paper has no clear purpose, and the writer includes limited, unclear, and irrelevant ideas.

Organization: The writer's organization is somewhat logical, although the paper still feels fragmentary and incomplete.

Voice: The writer seems unaware of the intended audience for the piece and uses a voice inappropriate for an essay in a school paper.

Word Choice: Word choice is limited, and occasionally words are misused.

Sentence Fluency: Sentences use a variety of structures but are often incomplete, run-on, or awkward.

Conventions: The numerous errors in grammar, punctuation, and spelling are distracting.

Presentation: The writer has taken care to present the essay neatly and clearly.

Portfolio Assessment

Portfolio Assessment in the Language Arts

Although establishing and using a portfolio assessment system requires a certain amount of time, effort, and understanding, an increasing number of teachers believe that the benefits of implementing such a system richly reward their efforts.

Language arts portfolios are collections of materials that display aspects of students' use of language. They are a means by which students can collect samples of their written work over time so that they and their teachers can ascertain how the students are developing as language users. Because reflection and self-assessment are built-in aspects of language arts portfolios, both also help students develop their critical-thinking and metacognitive abilities.

Each portfolio collection is typically kept in a folder, box, or other container to which items are added on a regular basis. The collection can include a great variety of materials, depending on the design of the portfolio assessment program, the kinds of projects completed inside and outside the classroom, and the interests of individual students. For example, portfolios may contain student stories, essays, sketches, poems, letters, journals, and other original writing, and they may also contain reactions to articles, stories, and other texts the student has read. Other materials that are suitable for inclusion in portfolios are drawings, photographs, audiotapes, and videotapes of students taking part in special activities; clippings and pictures from newspapers and magazines; and notes on favorite authors and on stories and books that the student hopes to read. Many portfolios also include several versions of the same piece of writing, demonstrating how the writing has developed through revision.

Finally, portfolios may contain logs of things the student has read or written, written reflections or assessments of portfolio work, and tables and explanations about the way the portfolio is organized. (A collection of forms that can be used to generate these items may be found at the end of this book.)

The Advantages of Portfolio Assessment

How can portfolio assessment help you meet your instructional goals? Here are some of the most important advantages of using portfolios:

- *Portfolios link instruction and assessment.* Traditional testing is usually one or more steps removed from the process or performance being assessed. However, because portfolio assessment focuses on performance—on students' actual use of language—portfolios are a highly accurate gauge of what students have learned in the classroom.

- *Portfolios involve students in assessing their own language use and abilities.* Portfolio assessment can provide some of the most effective learning opportunities available in your classroom. In fact, the assessment is

Portfolio Assessment in the Language Arts *(continued)*

itself instructional: Students, as self-assessors, identify their own strengths and weaknesses. Furthermore, portfolios are a natural way to develop metacognition in your students. As the collected work is analyzed, the student begins to think critically about how he or she makes meaning while reading, writing, speaking, and listening. For example, the student begins to ask questions while reading, such as "Is this telling me what I need to know?" "Am I enjoying this author as much as I expected to?" "Why or why not?" While writing, the student may ask, "Am I thinking about the goals I set when I was analyzing my portfolio?" That's what good instruction is all about: getting students to use the skills you help them develop.

- *Portfolios invite attention to important aspects of language.* Because most portfolios include numerous writing samples, they naturally direct attention to diction, style, main idea or theme, author's purpose, and other aspects of language that are difficult to assess in other ways. The portfolio encourages awareness and appreciation of these aspects of language as they occur in literature and nonfiction as well as in the student's own work.

- *Portfolios emphasize language use as a process that integrates language behaviors.* Students who keep and analyze portfolios develop an understanding that reading, writing, speaking, and listening are all aspects of a larger process. They come to see that language behaviors are connected by thinking about and expressing one's own ideas and feelings.

- *Portfolios make students aware of audience and the need for a writing purpose.* Students develop audience awareness by regularly analyzing their portfolio writing samples. Evaluation forms prompt them to reflect on whether they have defined and appropriately addressed their audience. Moreover, because portfolios provide or support opportunities for students to work together, peers can often provide feedback about how well a student has addressed an audience in his or her work. Finally, students may be asked to consider particular audiences (parents, classmates, or community groups, for example) who will review their portfolios; they may prepare explanations of the contents for such audiences, and they may select specific papers to present as a special collection to such audiences.

- *Portfolios provide a vehicle for student interaction and group learning.* Many projects that normally involve cooperative learning produce material for portfolios. Portfolios, in turn, provide or support many opportunities for students to work together. Students can work as

As they become attuned to audience, students automatically begin to be more focused on whether their work has fulfilled their purpose for writing. They begin to ask questions like, "Did I say what I meant to say? Could I have been clearer and more effective? Do I understand what this writer wants to tell me? Do I agree with it?" Speaking and listening activities can also be evaluated in terms of audience awareness and clarity of purpose.

PORTFOLIO ASSESSMENT

Portfolio Assessment in the Language Arts *(continued)*

partners or as team members who critique each other's collections. For example, students might work together to prepare, show, and explain portfolios to particular audiences, such as parents, administrators, and other groups interested in educational progress and accountability.

- *Portfolios can incorporate many types of student expression on a variety of topics.* Students should be encouraged to include materials from different subject areas and from outside school, especially materials related to hobbies and other special interests. In this way, students come to see language arts skills as crucial tools for authentic, real-world work.

- *Portfolios provide genuine opportunities to learn about students and their progress as language users.* Portfolio contents can reveal to the teacher a great deal about the student's background and interests with respect to reading, writing, speaking, and listening. Portfolios can also demonstrate the student's development as a language user and reveal areas where he or she needs improvement.

How to Develop and Use Portfolios

As you begin designing a portfolio program for your students, you may wish to read articles and reports that discuss the advantages of portfolio assessment.

You may want to require that certain papers, projects, and reports be included in the portfolio. Such requirements should be kept to a minimum so that students feel that they can include whatever they consider to be relevant to their language development.

Portfolios that include such planning papers and intermediate drafts are called *working portfolios*. Working portfolios force the student to organize and analyze the material collected, an activity that makes clear to the student that language use is a process.

Basic Design Features

For a portfolio program to be successful in the classroom, the program should reflect the teacher's particular instructional goals and the students' needs as learners. Teachers are encouraged to customize a portfolio program for their classrooms, although most successful portfolio programs share a core of essential portfolio management techniques. Following are suggestions that teachers will want to consider in customizing a portfolio program.

- *Integrate portfolio assessment into the regular classroom routine.* Teachers should make portfolio work a regular class activity by providing opportunities for students to work with their collections during class time. During these portfolio sessions, the teacher should promote analysis (assessment) that reflects his or her instructional objectives and goals.

- *Link the program to classroom activities.* Student portfolios should contain numerous examples of classroom activities and projects. To ensure that portfolios reflect the scope of students' work, some teachers require that certain papers and assignments be included.

- *Let students have the control.* Students can develop both self-assessment and metacognition skills when they select and arrange portfolio contents themselves. This practice also develops a strong sense of ownership: Students feel that their portfolios belong to them, not to the teacher. When students take ownership of their work, they accept more responsibility for their own language development. To encourage a sense of ownership on the part of students, portfolios should be stored where students can get at them easily, and students should have regular and frequent access to their portfolios.

- *Include students' creative efforts.* To ensure that the portfolios develop a range of language skills, encourage students to include samples of their creative writing, pieces they have written outside class, and publishing activities that they may have participated in, such as the production of a class magazine.

- *Make sure portfolios record students' writing process.* If portfolios are to teach language use as a process that integrates various language behaviors, they need to contain papers that show how writing grows out of planning and develops through revision. Portfolios should include notes, outlines, clippings, reactions to reading or oral presentations, pictures, and other materials that inspired the final product. Equally vital to the

How to Develop and Use Portfolios *(continued)*

The act of selecting particular papers to show to special audiences—parents, another teacher, or the principal, to name a few—refines students' sense of audience. Preparing and presenting selected collections, called *show portfolios*, engages students in a more sophisticated analysis of their work and encourages them to visualize the audience for the show collection.

If students feel free to include writing and reading done outside class in their portfolios, you can discover interests, opinions, and concerns that can be touched on during conferences. In turn, by communicating interest in and respect for what engages the student, you can promote the success of the portfolio program.

portfolio collections are the different drafts of papers that demonstrate revision over a period of time. Such collections can promote fruitful, concrete discussions between student and teacher about how the student's process shaped the final product.

- *Rely on reactions to reading and listening.* If portfolios are to link and interrelate language behaviors, students must be encouraged to include reactions to things they read and hear. During conferences, teachers may want to point out how some of the student's work has grown out of listening or reading.

- *Encourage students to consider the audience.* Portfolio building prompts students to think about the audience because, as a kind of publication, the portfolio invites a variety of readers. Students will become interested in and sensitive to the reactions of their classmates and their teacher, as well as to the impact of the collections on any other audiences that may be allowed to view them.

- *Promote collaborative products.* Portfolios can promote student collaboration if the program sets aside class time for students to react to one another's work and to work in groups. This interaction can occur informally or in more structured student partnerships or team responses. In addition, many writing projects can be done by teams and small groups, and any common product can be reproduced for all participants' portfolios. Performance projects, speeches, and other oral presentations often require cooperative participation. Audiotapes and videotapes of group projects may be included in portfolios.

- *Let the portfolios reflect a variety of subject areas and interests.* The language arts portfolio should include material from subject areas other than language arts. Broadening the portfolio beyond the language arts classroom is important if the student is to understand that reading, writing, speaking, and listening are authentic activities—that is, that they are central to all real-world activities. Any extensive attempt to limit portfolio contents may suggest to students that these activities are important only in the language arts classroom.

Initial Design Considerations

Using what you have read so far, you can make some initial notes as guidelines for drafting your portfolio assessment design. You can complete a chart like the one on the next page to plan how you will use portfolios and what you can do to make them effective.

How to Develop and Use Portfolios *(continued)*

▶ What are my primary goals in developing my students' ability to use language?	▶ How can portfolios contribute to meeting these goals?	▶ What design features can ensure this?

PORTFOLIO ASSESSMENT

How to Develop and Use Portfolios (*continued*)

Some key considerations for designing a portfolio program have been suggested. Other considerations will arise as you assess ways to use the portfolios. Here are some questions that will probably arise in the planning stages of portfolio assessment.

How can I introduce students to the concepts of portfolio management?

What examples of student work should go into the portfolios?

What should the criteria be for deciding what will be included?

How and where will the portfolio collections be kept?

Designing a Portfolio Program

How can I introduce students to the concepts of portfolio management?

One way to introduce students to portfolios is to experiment with a group of your students. If you use this limited approach, be sure to select students with varied writing abilities to get a sense of how portfolios work for students with a range of skill levels. To introduce portfolio assessment to them, you can talk to students either individually or as a group about what they will be doing. If other students begin expressing an interest in keeping portfolios, let them take part as well. The kind of excitement that builds around portfolio keeping almost guarantees that some students not included initially will want to get on board for the trial run; some may start keeping portfolios on their own.

You might let students help you design or at least plan some details of the system. After explaining both the reasons for keeping portfolios and the elements of the program that you have decided are essential, you can let students discuss how they think certain aspects should be handled. Even if you decide you want students to make important decisions concerning the program's design, you will need to have a clear idea of what your teaching objectives are and of what you will ask students to do.

What examples of student work should go into the portfolios?

Portfolios should reflect as much as possible the spectrum of your students' language use. What you want to ensure is that student self-assessment leads to the understanding that language skills are essential to all learning. For this to happen, portfolios should contain writing, speaking, and listening activities that relate to a number of subject areas and interests, not just to the language arts. Moreover, the portfolio should include final, completed works as well as drafts, notes, freewriting, and other samples that show the student's thinking and writing process.

FINAL PRODUCTS Students should consider including pieces that are created with a general audience in mind; writing that is communicative and intended for particular audiences; and writing that is very personal and that is used as a method of thinking through situations, evaluating experiences, or musing simply for enjoyment. The portfolios can contain a variety of finished products, including

- original stories, dialogue, and scripts
- poems

How to Develop and Use Portfolios *(continued)*

- essays, themes, sketches
- song lyrics
- original videos
- video or audio recordings of performances
- narrative accounts of experiences
- correspondence with family members and friends
- stream-of-consciousness pieces
- journals of various types

Examples of various types of journals that students might enjoy keeping are described below.

Keeping Journals

A journal is an excellent addition to a portfolio—and one that teachers report is very successful. Journal keeping develops the habit of recording one's observations, feelings, and ideas. At the same time, journal writing is an excellent way to develop fluency. Specifically, it can help tentative writers to overcome the reluctance to put thoughts down as words. Journal keeping can be a bridge over inhibitions to writing and can become a student's favorite example of his or her language use. These benefits support the addition of journals to the portfolio.

Success with journals in encouraging young writers has led teachers to experiment with a variety of types:

PERSONAL JOURNAL This form of journal allows the writer to make frequent entries (regularly or somewhat irregularly) on any topic and for any purpose. This popular and satisfying kind of journal writing develops writing fluency and reveals to students the essential relationship between thinking and writing. (If the journal is kept in the portfolio, you may wish to remind students that you will be viewing it. Tell students to omit anything they would not be comfortable sharing.)

LITERARY JOURNAL OR READER'S LOG This journal provides a way of promoting open-ended and freewheeling responses to student reading. Students are usually allowed to structure and organize these journals in any way that satisfies them. As a collection of written responses, the literary journal is a valuable source of notes for oral and written expression; it can also give students ideas for further reading. Finally, the literary journal is another tool that reveals to students that reading, writing, and thinking are interrelated.

TOPICAL JOURNAL This style of journal is dedicated to a particular interest or topic. It is a valuable experience for students to be allowed to express themselves freely about a specific topic—a favorite hobby, pastime, or issue, for example.

How to Develop and Use Portfolios *(continued)*

As with the literary journal, the topical journal can point students toward project ideas and further reading.

DIALOGUE JOURNAL For this journal format, students select one person—a classmate, friend, family member, or teacher, for example—with whom to have a continuing dialogue. Dialogue journals help develop audience awareness and can promote cooperative learning. If students in your class are keeping dialogue journals with each other, be prepared to help them decide in whose portfolio the journal will go. (Because making copies may be too time consuming or expensive, you could help students arrange alternate custody, or have them experiment by keeping two distinct journals.)

Fragments and Works in Progress

Portfolios should include, in addition to finished products, papers showing how your students are processing ideas as readers, writers, speakers, and listeners. Drafts that show how writing ideas are developed through revision are especially helpful as students assess their work. Items that demonstrate how your language users are working with their collections can include

- articles, news briefs, sketches, or other sources collected and used as the basis for written or oral projects. These sources may include pictures created or collected by students and used for inspiration for the subject.
- reading-response notes that have figured in the planning of a paper and have been incorporated into the final work. Some notes may be intended for future projects.
- other notes, outlines, or evidence of planning for papers written or ready to be drafted
- pieces in which the student is thinking out a problem, considering a topic of interest or behavior, or planning something for the future. These pieces may include pro and con arguments, persuasive points, and reactions to reading.
- freewriting, done either at school or at home
- early versions (drafts) of the latest revision of a piece of writing
- notes analyzing the student's latest draft, which may direct subsequent revision
- solicited reactions from classmates or the teacher
- a published piece accompanied by revised manuscripts showing edits

How to Develop and Use Portfolios *(continued)*

- correspondence from relatives and friends to which students have written a response or to which students need to respond
- journal or diary entries that are equivalent to preliminary notes or drafts of a piece of writing
- tapes of conversations or interviews to which a piece of writing refers or on which it is based

While test results in general do not make good contents for portfolios, performance assessments can provide a focused example of both language processing and integration of reading and writing skills. Such performance tests are now frequently structured as realistic tasks that require reading, synthesizing, and reacting to particular texts. More often than not, these assessments guide the student through planning stages and a preliminary draft. (These parts of the assessment are rarely rated, but they lend themselves directly to self-analysis and should definitely be included with the final draft.)

What should the criteria be for deciding what will be included?

Teachers often want to ensure that students keep certain kinds of papers in the portfolios, while also affirming students' need for a genuine sense of ownership of their collections. Achieving a balance between these two general objectives may not be as difficult as it seems. Students can be informed at the time that they are introduced to the portfolio concept that they will be asked to keep certain items as one part of the overall project. Almost certainly, it will be necessary to explain at some point that the collections are to be working portfolios and that certain records—including many of the forms provided in this booklet—will also need to be included. As they become accustomed to analyzing the papers in their portfolios, students can be encouraged or required to select the contents of their portfolios, using criteria that they develop themselves. Teachers can help students articulate these criteria in informal and formal conferences. Following are criteria teachers or students might consider:

- papers that students think are well done and that therefore represent their best efforts, or papers that were difficult to complete
- subjects that students enjoyed writing about, or texts they have enjoyed reading; things that they think are interesting or will interest others
- things that relate to reading or writing that students intend to do in the future, including ideas that may be developed into persuasive essays, details to support positions on issues, and reactions to favorite literary texts

Discourage the inclusion of workbook sheets, unless they contain ideas for future student writing; they tend to obscure the message that language development is a process, a major component of which is the expression of student ideas and opinions.

You might want to brainstorm a list of things that could be kept in your students' portfolios and then prioritize the items on your list according to which ones you think will be essential for students' development.

PORTFOLIO ASSESSMENT

How to Develop and Use Portfolios *(continued)*

- papers that contain ideas or procedures that students wish to remember
- incomplete essays or projects that presented some problem for the student. He or she may plan to ask a parent, teacher, or fellow student to react to the work or to earlier drafts.
- work that students would like particular viewers of the portfolio (the teacher, their parents, their classmates, and so on) to see, for some reason. This criterion is one that will dictate selections for a show portfolio; it may also determine some of the papers selected for the overall collection.

After building their collections for some time, students should be able to examine them and make lists of their selection criteria in their own words. Doing so should balance out any requirements the teacher has set for inclusion and should ensure students' sense of ownership.

A final note on selection criteria for student portfolios: While portfolios should certainly contain students' best efforts, too often teachers and students elect to collect only their "best stuff." An overemphasis on possible audiences that might view the collection can make it seem important that the collection be a show portfolio. Preparing show portfolios for particular audiences can require students to assess their work in order to decide what is worth including. That is a worthwhile experience, but once the preparation for the show has been completed, student self-assessment ends.

How and where will the portfolio collections be kept?

Part of the fun of keeping portfolios is deciding what the holders for the collections will look like. In a few classrooms, portfolio holders are standardized, but in most classes, the students are allowed to create their own. Many teachers allow students to furnish their own containers or folders, as long as these are big enough to hold the collections without students' having to fold or roll the papers—and not so large as to create storage problems. In addition, many teachers encourage their students to decorate their portfolio holders in unique, colorful, personal, and whimsical ways. Allowing this individuality creates enthusiasm for the project. It also helps students develop a genuine sense of ownership, an important attitude to foster if this system is to succeed.

The kinds of holders that students are likely to bring to school include household cardboard boxes, stationery boxes, folders of various types, paper or plastic shopping bags, computer paper boxes, and plastic and cardboard containers for storing clothing and other items. It would be a good idea to

> Start collecting some samples of holders you can show when you introduce portfolio management to your students. Decorate at least one sample, or have a young friend or relative do it. At the same time, be thinking about areas in your classroom where the collections can be kept.

How to Develop and Use Portfolios *(continued)*

have several different examples to show students when discussing how they will keep their papers. It is also a good idea to have some holders on hand for students who are unable to find anything at home that they think is suitable, and for use as replacements for unworkable holders some students may bring, such as shoe boxes that are too small to hold the portfolio items.

The resulting storage area will probably not be neatly uniform but will not necessarily be unattractive, either. Teachers who want a tidier storage area might find similar boxes to pass out to all students, who are then allowed to personalize them in different ways.

The amount of space available in a particular classroom will, of course, determine where students keep their collections, but it is vital that the area be accessible to students. It will save a great deal of inconvenience during the school year if the portfolios are on open shelves or on an accessible ledge of some kind and are not too far from students. If students can retrieve and put away their portfolios in less than a minute or two, there will be many instances when portfolio work can be allowed. Deciding where to keep the portfolios is a decision that may be put off until students know enough about the process to help make the decision.

Open access to portfolios does create the possibility of students looking at classmates' collections without permission and without warning. Remind students not to include in their portfolio anything they would not want others to see. A caution from the teacher could save a student from a wounding embarrassment.

Conferencing with Students

If you are new at conducting portfolio conferences, ask a student who has kept one or more papers to sit down and talk with you. Talk with the student about what he or she thinks is strong about the paper, how it came to be written, and what kind of reading or research the student undertook. See how well you can promote an open-ended conversation related to the topic of the paper and to language use.

The regular informal exchanges between teacher and student about portfolio content are obviously very important, but the more formal conferences that anchor a successful program are of equal if not greater importance. Conferences are evidence that both the teacher and the student take the portfolio collection seriously and that the usefulness of the portfolio depends on an ongoing analysis of it. By blocking out time to conduct at least four formal conferences with each student each year, the teacher demonstrates a commitment to the program and a genuine interest in each student's progress.

Conducting Portfolio Conferences

The conference should proceed as a friendly but clearly directed conversation between the student and the teacher. The focus of the conference should be on how the use of language serves the student's needs and interests. This focus translates, in the course of the conference, into helping each student reflect on why and how he or she reads and writes.

Think about what you could do to ensure a productive portfolio conference that would be helpful and worthwhile to students.

Teachers will want to discuss with students the quantity of recent writing compared with that of previous time periods, the kinds of writing that the student has done, and the student's purposes for writing. Teachers will also want to discuss how the inclusions in the portfolio came to be and whether the pieces represent experiences and ideas the student has enjoyed and thinks are important. Teachers should let students know that the portfolio documents say something important about the individual student's life. In fact, a significant portion of the conference may be dedicated to learning about the student's interests. Here are a few examples of the types of statements that might elicit a helpful response:

- You seem to know a lot about deep-sea diving.
- Where did you learn all those details?
- Have you looked for books about deep-sea diving?
- What kinds of things could you write about deep-sea diving?

The student, too, should feel free to ask questions:

- Which pieces seem the best to the teacher and why?
- Is it always necessary to write for an audience?
- What if I *want* an idea or thought to remain private, though written?
- If I don't know how to spell a certain word, is it OK to just keep writing and look it up later?

PORTFOLIO ASSESSMENT

Conferencing with Students *(continued)*

These examples show how the conference can provide power-ful, effective opportunities to teach and to guide language development. The conference conversations between the teacher and the student should be as unique as the individual student who joins the teacher in this exchange.

Ideally, each student will look forward to the conference as a time when student and teacher pay close attention to what the student has done; how the student feels about that perfor-mance; and what the student's needs and goals are. Such con-ferences encourage students to accept responsibility for their own development.

The following guidelines will help the teacher make the most of portfolio conferences.

Conference Guidelines

- *Conferences should be conducted without interruption.* Plan creatively: Perhaps a volunteer assistant can man-age the rest of the class during meetings. Or, assign to other students learning activities or other work that does not disrupt your exchange with the student. It may be necessary to conduct the conference outside class time.

- *Keep the focus on the student.* Make the conference as much like an informal conversation as possible by ask-ing questions that will emphasize the student's inter-ests, attitudes toward writing, and favorite topics. Demonstrate that you care about what the student thinks and likes. You can also show that you respect the way a student's individuality is manifested in language use.

- *Let the conversation develop naturally.* Be an active lis-tener: Give full attention to what the student is saying. The student's contribution is likely to suggest a ques-tion or comment from you, resulting in a genuine and natural exchange. There may be opportunities to get back to questions you had hoped to ask, but teachers should respect the course that the exchange takes and realize that some of their planned questions will need to be dropped. Good listening on the part of the teacher will help create successful conferences that address indi-vidual student interests and needs.

- *Be sincere but not judgmental.* Avoid evaluating or passing judgment on interests or aspects of the student's language use. On the other hand, try to avoid continu-ally expressing approval and thereby creating a situa-tion in which the student tries to respond in a way that will win favor: The conference will then lose its focus on the individual's language needs and development.

For many teachers, the time and planning that the conference demands constitute the most difficult aspect of portfolio assessment. Think about how you can use all the resources at your dis-posal, and don't forget to enlist students' help. Ask them to help you schedule meetings, and request their cooperation so that the system functions smoothly.

Questions will undoubtedly occur to you while reviewing the student's port-folio. It may be useful to have a few notes to remind you of things you would like to ask. Do not, however, approach a conference with a list that dictates the exchange with the student.

PORTFOLIO ASSESSMENT

Conferencing with Students *(continued)*

Don't hesitate to use the conference as a means of getting to know the student better by learning about his or her interests, pastimes, concerns, and opinions. This can be time well spent, particularly if it demonstrates to the student that the various aspects of his or her life can be very closely connected to the use and development of language arts skills.

Shortly after the conference, the student can translate his or her notes to a worksheet like the goal-setting form in this book, which will ask the student to elaborate on the objectives that have been established.

- ■ *Keep the conversation open and positive.* It is fine to ask questions that direct the focus back to the collection, as long as that leads in turn to a discussion of ideas and content, the process of writing, and indications of the student's strengths and progress as a language user. In general, however, teachers should ask questions that promise to open up discussion, not shut it down. Phrase questions and comments so that they invite elaboration and explanation.

- ■ *Gear the conference toward goal setting.* Identify and come to an agreement about the goals and objectives the student will be working on during the next time period.

- ■ *Limit the attention devoted to usage errors.* If the student needs to focus on mechanical or grammatical problems, suggest that over the next time period the student pay particular attention to these problems when editing and revising. Do not, however, turn the session into a catalogue of language errors encountered. Keep in mind that if there are four conferences and each one tactfully encourages a focus on just one or two examples of nonstandard usage, it is possible to eliminate from four to eight high-priority errors during the course of a school year.

- ■ *Keep joint notes with the student on the conference.* To keep a focus on the most important aspects of the conference, you and the student should keep notes. Frequently, student and teacher will record notes based on the same observation: For example, the student might write, "I like to use a lot of verbs at the beginning of my sentences, but maybe I use too many." And the teacher might write, "Let's watch to see how often Cody frontshifts sentence elements for emphasis." The student might write, "Look for a novel about the Civil War." The teacher might note, "Find a copy of *The Killer Angels* for Cody if possible." When the two participants make notes on the same sheet, side by side, the notes on the same point will roughly correspond. The teacher and the student can even write at the same time if they can position the note sheet in a way that will facilitate this.

Keep in mind that conference notes frequently serve as a reference point for an action plan that is then more fully considered on the goal-setting worksheet.

Types of Student-Teacher Conferences

In addition to the scheduled conference, there are several other types of conferences that teachers can conduct as a part of portfolio assessment:

Conferencing with Students *(continued)*

GOAL CLARIFICATION CONFERENCES If a student appears to be having trouble using the portfolio system, a goal clarification conference can be scheduled. The meeting's focus should be to help the student clarify and articulate objectives so that work on the collection is directed and productive.

It is important that this session not be perceived as being overly critical of the student. Be supportive and positive about the collection; try to generate a discussion that will lead to clear goals for the student. These objectives can be articulated on a goal-setting worksheet, which the teacher can help the student fill out.

PUBLICATION STAFF CONFERENCES Students who are publishing pieces they write may frequently meet as teams or in staff conferences to select pieces from their portfolios. They may also discuss possible revisions of manuscripts they hope to publish. Teachers may enjoy observing and even participating in these but should let students direct them as much as possible.

Other class projects and collaborative activities can generate similar student conferences that may involve portfolio collections.

INFORMAL OR ROVING CONFERENCES In these conferences, teachers consult with students about their portfolios during impromptu sessions. For example, at any time a teacher might encounter a student with an important and intriguing question, or spot confusion or a situation developing into frustration for a self-assessor. Often the situation calls for effective questioning and then good listening, just as in the regularly scheduled conferences.

Questions and Answers

The questions that follow are frequently asked by teachers who are thinking about instituting a portfolio management system.

- How can I make my students familiar and comfortable with the idea of creating portfolios?
- How often should my students work on their portfolios?
- How can I keep the portfolios from growing too bulky to manage and analyze effectively?
- Should I grade my students' portfolios?
- Who else, besides the student and me, should be allowed to see the portfolio?
- How can I protect against the possible negative effects of allowing a wide variety of persons to see students' portfolios?

How can I make my students comfortable with portfolios?

Teachers will, of course, want to begin by describing what portfolios are and what they are designed to accomplish. One way to help students visualize portfolios is to point out that some professionals keep portfolios:

- Artists usually keep portfolios to show prospective clients or employers what kind of work they can do. In a sense, an artist's studio is one big working portfolio, full of projects in various stages of completion.
- Photographers, architects, clothing designers, interior designers, and a host of other professionals keep portfolios full of samples of their work.
- Models carry portfolios of pictures showing them in a variety of styles and situations.
- Some writers keep portfolios of their work.
- People who invest their money in stocks and bonds call the collection of different investments they hold a portfolio.

Teachers can encourage students' interest by inviting to the classroom someone who can exhibit and explain a professional portfolio. Teachers might also show students an actual language arts portfolio created by a student in another class or school. Some teachers put together a portfolio of their own and use it as an example for their students.

After this or another introduction, you might share the following information with students:

- Explain what kinds of things will go into the portfolios and why. Students can choose what to include in their collections, but teachers can indicate that a few items will be required, including some records. Without introducing all the records to be used, teachers might show and explain basic forms, such as logs. If forms filled out by students are available, use them as examples.

Questions and Answers *(continued)*

- Stress that portfolios will be examined regularly. If the working portfolios will be available to parents or others, be sure to inform students. If you plan for others to see only show portfolios, this might be a good time to introduce this kind of portfolio.
- Show examples of holders that might be used, and explain where they will be kept. Students can be involved in making decisions about how and where portfolios will be housed.

How often should my students work on their portfolios?

The answer is "regularly and often." Teachers should schedule half-hour sessions weekly; ideally, there will be time almost every day when students can work on their collections. The Scheduling Plan on the next page shows activities that should occur regularly in your program.

How can I keep the portfolios from growing too bulky to manage and analyze effectively?

Because portfolios are intended to demonstrate students' products and processes over time, collections should be culled only when necessary. However, working portfolios can become simply too big, bulky, and clumsy to organize and analyze. If some students find their collections too unwieldy to work with, encourage them to try one of the following techniques:

- Cull older pieces except for those that stand as the best work examples. Put the removed contents into a separate holder and complete an *About My Portfolio* record. Explain on the record that the work consists of less-favored work, and have students take it home for parents to examine and/or save. Photocopies of later work that you consider more successful can be included as comparison.
- Close the whole collection, except for writing not yet completed, notes and records the student intends to use, and other idea files. Send the entire collection home with an explanation record, and start a new portfolio.
- Cull from the collection one or more show portfolios for particular audiences, such as parents, other relatives, other teachers, administrators, or supervisors. After the show portfolio has been viewed, return it to the rest of the collection. Start a new portfolio, beginning with the ideas in progress.

Some teachers have their students prepare a larger decorated box to take home at the beginning of the school year. This container eventually holds banded groups of papers culled during the year. Students then have one repository for their entire portfolio collection, which they can keep indefinitely.

Questions and Answers *(continued)*

SCHEDULING PLAN FOR PORTFOLIO ASSESSMENT

Activity	Frequency	The Student	The Teacher
Keeping logs	As writing and other language experiences are completed; daily if necessary	Makes the entries on the *Record of My Writing*	Encourages the student to make regular entries and discusses with the student indications of progress, developing interests, etc.
Collecting writing samples, reactions to reading, entries that reflect on oral language	As drafts and reactions to reading become available; can be as often as daily	Selects materials to be included	Can select materials to be included; may require some inclusions
Keeping journal(s)	Ongoing basis; daily to at least once a week	Makes regular entries in one or more journals	Analyzes journal writing discreetly and confidentially
Adding notes, pictures, clippings, and other idea sources	Weekly or more often	Clips and collects ideas and adds them to appropriate place in the portfolio	Reacts to student's idea sources (every month or so); discusses with student how he or she will use them
Explaining, analyzing, evaluating inclusions	Weekly; at least every other week	Uses forms for evaluating and organizing work to analyze and describe individual pieces included	Analyzes inclusions and student analysis of them at least four times a year—before conferences
Completing summary analyses	Monthly and always before conference	Completes a *Summary of My Progress* record while comparing it with previously completed summary	Completes selected progress reports at least four times a year—before conferences, relying on student summaries and previously completed records
Conferencing—informal	Ongoing; ideally, at least once a week	Freely asks teacher for advice as often as needed; shares emerging observations with teacher	Makes an effort to observe student working on portfolio at least every two weeks and to discuss one or more specific new inclusions and analyses
Conferencing—formal	At least four times a year	Prepares for conference by completing summaries; discusses portfolio contents and analysis of them with teacher; devises new goals; takes joint notes	Prepares for conference with evaluative analyses; discusses portfolio contents and analysis with student; establishes new goals; takes joint notes
Preparing explanation of portfolio and analysis of it for a particular audience	As occasion for allowing other audiences access arises	Thoughtfully fills out the *About My Portfolio* form	Keeps student advised as to when other audiences might be looking at the student's collection and who the viewer(s) will be
Reacting to a fellow student's paper or portfolio	When it is requested by a "partner" or other classmate	Conferences with peer	Encourages collaboration whenever possible

PORTFOLIO ASSESSMENT

Should I grade my students' portfolios?

Teachers might be tempted to grade portfolios to let students know that they are accountable for their work; teachers may also feel that a grade legitimizes—or at least recognizes—the time and effort that goes into successful portfolio assessment. Finally, many parents, school supervisors, and administrators will expect the teacher to grade the portfolio. These reasons notwithstanding, most portfolio experts recommend that portfolios not be graded. Keep in mind that the collection will contain papers that have been graded. A grade for the collection as a whole, however, risks undermining the goals of portfolio management. Grading portfolios may encourage students to include only their "best" work, and that practice may convey the message that student self-assessment is not taken seriously. Think about it: How would you feel if someone decided to incorporate your journal entries, your collection of ideas that interest you, and other notes and informal jottings into a package that was being rated and given a grade?

Who, besides the student and me, should see the portfolio?

This question raises some of the same concerns as the issue of grading portfolios. Teachers may feel some responsibility to let parents, a supervisor, the principal, and fellow faculty members know how the program is proceeding and what it shows about the progress of individuals or of the class as a whole. It is important to balance the benefits of showing portfolios to outside audiences against the possible adverse effects—the risk of inhibiting students, diminishing their sense of ownership, or invading their privacy. Above all, the primary aims of portfolio assessment must be kept in mind.

Following are some suggestions for showing portfolios, with respect to the audience involved.

Another way to involve parents in portfolio management is to let students plan a workshop on portfolio management geared for parents and others who are interested. Or, as suggested earlier, have students cull their collections periodically and take the materials home for their parents to see.

PARENTS OR GUARDIANS Family members will almost certainly be viewing the portfolio in one form or another. If parents or other responsible adults are to view collections only on more formal occasions, such as back-to-school night or during unscheduled visits to the classroom, then students should be assisted in creating show portfolios. If, on the other hand, the teacher will show students' portfolios without the owners' knowledge or without offering them the opportunity to review the contents beforehand, the teacher must tell students this at the beginning of the year. Warning students of these unscheduled viewings may qualify their sense of ownership; it can also intensify their audience awareness.

PORTFOLIO ASSESSMENT

Questions and Answers *(continued)*

Again, if portfolios will be shown to other educators, students should be made aware of this before they start to build their collections.

SCHOOL SUPERVISORS AND PRINCIPALS Students' portfolios can demonstrate to fellow educators how youngsters develop as language users, thinkers, and people; they can also show the kind of learning that is taking place in the classroom. When working portfolios are shown, they are usually selected at random from those kept in the class, and the owner's identity is masked. Show portfolios are usually prepared specifically for this purpose. Whether teachers use working or show collections (assuming the state or school system does not mandate one) may depend partly on whether they think the audience will be able to appreciate that the working collections show process.

CLASSMATES Students may review their peers' portfolios as part of the program's assessment. Even if a particular program does not include a formal peer-review stage, remind students that peers may see their collections—either in the process of collaborative work or peer review, or because a student does not respect the privacy of others.

NEXT YEAR'S TEACHERS At the end of the school year, teachers can help students create a show portfolio for their next teacher or teachers. These portfolios should demonstrate the student's growth during the year and the potential of his or her best efforts. They should also indicate the most recent goals established by the teacher and the student, so that the new teacher knows how the student sees his or her language skills developing over the next year.

Encourage students to include finished projects as well as earlier drafts. Discuss what kinds of logs should be included, or have students prepare a brief report showing how goals have been met. A fresh table of contents would be useful, as would an explanation of what the show collection includes and what its purpose is. Teachers may want to let students make copies of some papers that they would also like to take home.

THE STUDENTS THEMSELVES At the end of the school year, portfolio contents can be sent home for parents to see and save, if they wish. Before doing this, teachers may wish to have students prepare a starter portfolio of ideas, writing, plans for reading, and so on, for next year.

How can I protect against the possible negative effects of allowing a wide variety of persons to see students' portfolios?

Whatever special reporting the teacher does with portfolios, he or she needs to offset any possible adverse effects by keeping the primary aims for portfolio assessment in mind.

Questions and Answers *(continued)*

- The overall goal of the program is to develop students as language users. That goal should become the focus of joint student/teacher evaluation of the student's progress.
- Because another important goal is for students to develop a habit of self-assessment, the collections must be readily available to students.
- The emphasis should be on examining the process by looking at the product and the way it is produced. Each portfolio should be a working collection containing notes, drafts, and records of the evaluation of its contents.
- The activities assessed should integrate reading, writing, speaking, and listening.
- The portfolio should be controlled and owned by the student.
- The collections should include reactions to and applications of a variety of text and writing types—with a variety of purposes involving different audiences.

Table of Contents: How My Portfolio Is Organized

Decide on the major categories for work in your portfolio. Then, in the sections below, list the categories you have chosen. The works themselves may be papers, speech notecards, videotapes, multimedia products, or any work you and your teacher agree should be included. In choosing categories, consider organizing work by topic, by genre (essays, poems, stories, and so on), by chronology (work completed by month, for example), by level of difficulty (work that was less difficult, somewhat difficult, and more difficult), or according to another plan.

Grade: _____ **School year:** _____

▶ WORK IN EACH SECTION	▶ WHY I PUT THIS WORK IN THIS SECTION
Section 1:	
title:	
title:	
title:	
title:	
Section 2:	
title:	
title:	
title:	
Section 3:	
title:	
title:	
title:	
title:	

PORTFOLIO ASSESSMENT

About My Portfolio

Use this form whenever you are preparing your portfolio for review by your teacher or another reader.

Grade: _____ **School year:** _____ **When I began this portfolio:** _____

▶ **How it is organized:**

_____

▶ **What I think it shows about my progress . . .**

as a reader:

_____

as a writer:

_____

as a listener:

_____

as a speaker:

GO ON ➡

About My Portfolio *(continued)*

▶ **Examples of My Best Work**

The best things I have read are—	Why I like them—

The best things I have written are—	Why I like them—

Other things in my portfolio that I hope you notice are—	What they show—
1.	
2.	
3.	

TO PARENT OR GUARDIAN

Home Review: What the Portfolio Shows

In the left-hand column of the chart below, I have noted what I believe this portfolio shows about your child's development in areas such as reading, writing, speaking, and listening. The right-hand column notes where you can look for evidence of that development.

    A prime objective in keeping portfolios is to develop in students a habit of analyzing and evaluating their work. This portfolio includes work that the student has collected over a period of time. The student has decided what to include but has been encouraged to include different types of writing, responses to reading, and evidence of other uses of language. Many of the writings included are accompanied by earlier drafts and plans that show how the work has evolved from a raw idea to a finished piece of writing. The inclusion of drafts is intended to reinforce to the student that using language entails a process of revision and refinement.

▶ I believe that this portfolio shows—	▶ To see evidence of this, please notice—

Teacher's signature_____

PORTFOLIO ASSESSMENT

TO PARENT OR GUARDIAN

Home Response to the Portfolio

▶ Please answer any questions that seem important to you. Use the reverse side for any additional comments or questions.

Parent or Guardian _____ Date _____

What did you learn from the portfolio about your child's reading?

_____

_____

_____

What did you learn from the portfolio about your child's writing?

_____

_____

_____

Were you surprised by anything in the portfolio? Why?

_____

_____

What do you think is the best thing in the portfolio? What do you like about it?

_____

_____

_____

Do you have questions about anything in the portfolio? What would you like to know more about?

_____

_____

_____

What does the portfolio tell you about your child's progress as a writer, reader, and thinker?

_____

_____

_____

Do you think keeping a portfolio has had an effect on your child as a reader or writer—or in another way? If so, what?

_____

_____

_____

_____

Is there anything missing from the portfolio that you would have liked or had expected to see? If so, what?

_____

_____

PORTFOLIO ASSESSMENT

SELF-EVALUATION

Record of My Writing

> **Ratings:** ✓✓✓✓ One of my best!   ✓✓ OK, but not my best
>   ✓✓✓ Better if I revise it   ✓ I don't like this one.

▶ Month/ Day	▶ Title and type of writing	▶ Notes about this piece of writing	▶ Rating

PORTFOLIO ASSESSMENT

SELF-EVALUATION

My Spelling Log

▶ Word	▶ My misspelling	▶ How to remember correct spelling

Goal-Setting for Writing, Listening, and Speaking

GOAL	STEPS TO REACH GOAL	REVIEW OF PROGRESS
Writing Goals		

GO ON ➡

PORTFOLIO ASSESSMENT

Goal-Setting for Writing, Listening, and Speaking *(continued)*

GOAL	STEPS TO REACH GOAL	REVIEW OF PROGRESS
Listening Goals		
Speaking Goals		

Summary of My Progress: Writing, Listening, and Speaking

Complete this form before sitting down with your teacher or a classmate to assess your overall progress, set goals, or discuss specific pieces of your work.

Grade : _____   **School year:** _____   **Date of summary:** _____

▶ **What work have I done so far this year?**

Writing:

Listening:

Speaking:

▶ **What project do I plan to work on next?**

Writing:

Listening:

Speaking:

▶ **What do I think of my progress?**

What about my work has improved?

What needs to be better?

▶ **Which examples of work are my favorites and why?**

Summary of My Progress: Writing, Listening, and Speaking *(continued)*

▶ **Which pieces of work need more revision, and what is needed?**

▶ **How has listening or speaking helped me in preparing for papers or other projects this year?**

▶ **What a classmate or the teacher thinks about my progress**

In writing—

In listening—

In speaking—

PORTFOLIO ASSESSMENT

Inventory: Some Facts About My Writing

▶ Questions and answers about my writing	▶ More about my answers
How often do I write?	What types of writing do I do?
Where, besides school, do I write?	What kind of writing do I do there?
Do I like to write?	Why or why not?
Of the things I have written, I like these best:	Why do I like them best?
What topics do I like to write about?	Why do I like to write about these topics?
Is anything about writing difficult for me? What?	Why do I think it is difficult?
Does reading help me to be a better writer or vice versa?	Why do I think this?
How important is learning to write well?	Why do I think this?

NAME ______________________ CLASS ______________ DATE ______________

SELF-EVALUATION

Evaluating Your Writing Process: Analytic

Choose one paper from your portfolio, preferably one for which you have your prewriting notes and all your drafts. Use the chart below to analyze your writing process. Circle the numbers that most clearly indicate how well you meet the stated criteria in your writing process. The lowest possible total score is 5, the highest, 20.

1 = Do not meet these criteria

2 = Attempt to meet these criteria but need to improve

3 = Are fairly successful in meeting criteria

4 = Clearly meet these criteria

Title of paper ______________________________

STAGE IN WRITING PROCESS	CRITERIA FOR EVALUATION	RATING
Prewriting	▪ Use prewriting techniques to find and limit subject and to gather details about subject ▪ Organize details in a reasonable way	1 2 3 4
Writing	▪ Get most of ideas down on paper in a rough draft	1 2 3 4
Revising	▪ Do complete peer- or self-evaluation ▪ Find ways to improve content, organization, and style of rough draft ▪ Revise by adding, cutting, replacing, and moving material	1 2 3 4
Proofreading	▪ Correct errors in spelling, grammar, usage, punctuation, capitalization, and manuscript form	1 2 3 4
Publishing and Reflecting	▪ Produce a clean final copy in proper form ▪ Share the piece of writing with others ▪ Reflect on the writing process and on the paper's strengths and weaknesses	1 2 3 4

Additional Comments:

PORTFOLIO ASSESSMENT

SELF-EVALUATION

Proofreading Strategies

Proofread your paper using one of the following steps. Put a check by the step you used.

_____ **1.** Read the paper backward word by word.

_____ **2.** Make a large card with a one- or two-inch-sized strip cut into it and read every word in the paper, one at a time, through the hole.

_____ **3.** Read the first sentence in your paper carefully. Put your left index finger on the punctuation mark that signals the end of that sentence. Now, put your right index finger on the punctuation mark that ends the second sentence. Carefully read the material between your fingers; then, move your left index finger to the end of the second sentence and your right to the end of the third sentence, and read carefully. Keep moving your fingers until you have carefully examined each sentence in the paper.

List the mistakes you discovered when proofreading.

_____

_____

_____

_____

_____

_____

_____

_____

_____

_____

_____

_____

_____

_____

_____

PORTFOLIO ASSESSMENT

Proofreading Checklist

Read through the paper and then mark the following statements either **T** for true or **F** for false. If you are reviewing a classmate's paper, return the paper and checklist to the writer. After the writer has done his or her best to correct the paper, offer to assist if your help is needed.

Writer's name _____ **Title of paper**_____

_____ **1.** The paper is neat.

_____ **2.** Each sentence begins with a capital letter.

_____ **3.** Each sentence ends with a period, question mark, or exclamation mark.

_____ **4.** Each sentence is complete. Each has a subject and a predicate and expresses a complete thought.

_____ **5.** Run-on sentences are avoided.

_____ **6.** A singular verb is used with each singular subject and a plural verb with each plural subject.

_____ **7.** Nominative case pronouns such as *I* and *we* are used for subjects; objective case pronouns such as *me* and *us* are used for objects.

_____ **8.** Singular pronouns are used to refer to singular nouns, and plural pronouns are used to refer to plural nouns.

_____ **9.** Indefinite pronoun references are avoided.

_____ **10.** Each word is spelled correctly.

_____ **11.** Frequently confused words, such as *lie/lay, sit/set, rise/raise, all ready/already,* and *fewer/less,* are used correctly.

_____ **12.** Double negatives are avoided.

_____ **13.** All proper nouns and proper adjectives are capitalized.

_____ **14.** Word endings such as *–s, –ing,* and *–ed* are included where they should be.

_____ **15.** No words have been accidentally left out or accidentally written twice.

_____ **16.** Each paragraph is indented.

_____ **17.** Apostrophes are used correctly with contractions and possessive nouns.

_____ **18.** Commas or pairs of commas are used correctly.

_____ **19.** Dialogue is punctuated and capitalized correctly.

_____ **20.** Any correction that could not be rewritten or retyped is crossed out with a single line.

Record of Proofreading Corrections

Keeping a record of the kinds of mistakes you make can be helpful. For the next few writing assignments, list the errors you, your teacher, or your peers find in your work. If you faithfully use this kind of record, you'll find it easier to avoid troublesome errors.

Writer's name _____ **Title of paper** _____

Write sentences that contain errors in grammar or usage here.

Write corrections here.

_____ _____

_____ _____

_____ _____

_____ _____

_____ _____

Write sentences that contain errors in mechanics here.

Write corrections here.

_____ _____

_____ _____

_____ _____

_____ _____

_____ _____

_____ _____

Write misspelled words and corrections here.

_____ _____ _____ _____

_____ _____ _____ _____

_____ _____ _____ _____

_____ _____ _____ _____

SELF-EVALUATION

My Multiple-Assignment Proofreading Record

▶ **DIRECTIONS:** When your teacher returns a corrected writing assignment, write the title or topic on the appropriate vertical line at right. Under the title or topic, record the number of errors you made in each area. Use this sheet when you proofread your next assignment, taking care to check those areas in which you make frequent mistakes.

▶ **TITLE OR TOPIC OF ASSIGNMENT**

Type of Error									
Sentence Fragments									
Run-on Sentences									
Subject-Verb Agreement									
Pronoun Agreement									
Incorrect Pronoun Form									
Use of Double Negative									
Comparison of Adjectives and Adverbs									
Confusing Verbs									
Irregular Verbs									
Noun Plurals and Possessives									
Capitalization									
Spelling									
End Punctuation									
Apostrophes									
Confusing Words									
Quotation Marks and Italics									
Comma or Paired Commas									

PORTFOLIO ASSESSMENT

Inventory: Some Facts About My Listening

▶ Questions and answers about my listening	▶ More about my answers
What kinds of music do I like to listen to?	Why do I like them?
What TV shows and movies are my favorites?	What do I like about them?
How well do I listen in school?	How much do I learn by listening?
Do I listen carefully to what my friends say?	What do I learn from them?
When is it difficult for me to listen?	What makes it difficult?
How do I use the praise and suggestions of others to improve my skills?	How do I feel about getting praise or suggestions for improvement?

Inventory: Some Facts About My Speaking

▶ Questions and answers about my speaking	▶ More about my answers
How do I feel about speaking to friends?	What do I like to discuss with them?
How do I feel about talking to adults?	Why do I feel this way?
How do I feel about reciting or speaking to the class?	Why do I feel this way?
What is the most difficult thing about speaking?	Why is it difficult?
What techniques have I learned to improve my speaking?	How do I use these techniques with friends or in class?

PORTFOLIO ASSESSMENT

Skills Profile

Student's Name _____ **Grade** _____

Teacher's Name _____ **Date** _____

For each skill, write the date the observation is made and any comments that explain the student's development toward skills mastery.

SKILL	NOT OBSERVED	EMERGING	PROFICIENT
Writing			
Writing Modes			
Write a short story.			
Write a problem-solution essay.			
Write a personal narrative.			
Write a descriptive essay.			

Skills Profile *(continued)*

SKILL	NOT OBSERVED	EMERGING	PROFICIENT
Write an essay supporting an interpretation.			
Write a comparison-contrast essay.			
Write an informative report.			
Writing Process			
Prewriting			
• Choose a topic.			
• Identify purpose and audience.			

Skills Profile *(continued)*

SKILL	► NOT OBSERVED	► EMERGING	► PROFICIENT
• Generate ideas and gather information about the topic.			
• Begin to organize the information.			
• Draft a thesis statement, or a sentence that expresses the main point.			
Writing a Draft			
• State the main points and include relevant support and elaboration.			
• Follow a plan of organization.			

Skills Profile *(continued)*

SKILL	▶ NOT OBSERVED	▶ EMERGING	▶ PROFICIENT
Revising			
• Revise for content and style.			
Publishing			
• Proofread for grammar, usage, and mechanics.			
• Publish the work, or share the finished writing with readers.			
▶ **Listening and Speaking**			
Deliver a public-service announcement.			
Present a personal narrative.			

Skills Profile *(continued)*

SKILL	▶ NOT OBSERVED	▶ EMERGING	▶ PROFICIENT
Deliver a persuasive speech.			
Deliver an informative speech.			
Deliver a poetry reading.			
Conduct an interview.			
Analyze and evaluate speeches and oral presentations.			

Skills Profile *(continued)*

SKILL	▶ NOT OBSERVED	▶ EMERGING	▶ PROFICIENT
Plan and organize the speech or presentation.			
Rehearse and deliver the presentation.			
Use effective verbal and nonverbal techniques.			
Use visual aids.			
Evaluate content, organization, delivery, speaker's purpose, credibility, and overall effect of presentation.